"Ryan Holiday is one of his generation's finest thinkers, and this book is his best yet."

—STEVEN PRESSFIELD, author of *The War of Art*

"The comedian Bill Hicks said the world was tainted with fevered egos. In *Ego Is the Enemy*, Ryan Holiday writes us all a prescription: humility. This book is packed with stories and quotes that will help you get out of your own way. Whether you're starting out or starting over, you'll find something to steal here."

—AUSTIN KLEON, author of *Steal Like an Artist*

"This is a book I want every athlete, aspiring leader, entrepreneur, thinker, and doer to read. Ryan Holiday is one of the most promising young writers of his generation."

—GEORGE RAVELING, Hall of Fame Basketball coach and Nike's Director of International Basketball

"I see the toxic vanity of ego at play every day and it never ceases to amaze me how often it wrecks promising creative endeavors. Read this book before it wrecks you or the projects and people you love. Consider it as urgently as you do a proper workout regimen and eating right. Ryan's insights are priceless."

—MARC ECKO, founder of Ecko Unltd and Complex

"I don't have many rules in life, but one I never break is: If Ryan Holiday writes a book, I read it as soon as I can get my hands on it."

—BRIAN KOPPELMAN, screenwriter and director of *Rounders, Ocean's Thirteen,* and *Billions*

"In his new book Ryan Holiday attacks the greatest obstacle to mastery and true success in life—our insatiable ego. In an inspiring yet practical way, he teaches us how to manage and tame this beast within us so that we can focus on what really matters—producing the best work possible."

—ROBERT GREENE, author of *Mastery*

"We're often told that to achieve success, we need confidence. With refreshing candor, Ryan Holiday challenges that assumption, highlighting how we can earn confidence by pursuing something bigger than our own success."

—ADAM GRANT, author of *Originals* and *Give and Take*

"Once again Ryan Holiday has laid down the gauntlet for readers willing to challenge themselves with the tough questions of our time. Every reader will find truths that are pertinent to each of our lives. Ego can be the enemy if we are unarmed with the cautionary insights of history, scripture, and philosophy. As was said to St. Augustine more than a thousand years ago, 'Pick it up and read'; for to not do so is to allow the enemy to bring despair."

—DR. DREW PINSKY, host of HLN's *Dr. Drew On Call* and *Loveline*

"In this day and age where everyone seeks instant gratification, the idea of success is skewed—many believing the road to their goals is a linear path. As a former professional athlete I can tell you that the road is anything but linear. In fact, it is one that consists of twists, turns, and ups and downs—it requires you to put your head down and put in the work. Ryan Holiday hits the nail on the head with this book, reminding us that the real success is in the journey and learning process. I only wish I had had this gem as a reference during my playing days."

— LORI LINDSEY, former U.S. Women's National Team soccer player

"Philosophy has gotten a bad rap, but Ryan Holiday is restoring it to its rightful place in our lives. This book—packed with unforgettable stories, strategies, and lessons—is perfect for anyone who strives to do and accomplish. It's no exaggeration to say that, after finishing it, you'll never open your laptop and sit down to work the same way again."

— JIMMY SONI, Former Managing Editor of *The Huffington Post* and author of *Rome's Last Citizen*

"I would like to rip out every page and use them as wallpaper so I could be reminded constantly of the humility and work it takes to truly succeed. In the margins of my copy, I have scrawled the same message over and over—'pre-Gold.' Reading this inspiring book brought me back to the humility and work ethic it took to win the Olympics."

— CHANDRA CRAWFORD, Olympic Gold Medalist

"What a valuable book for those in positions of authority! It has made me a better judge."

— THE HONORABLE FREDERIC BLOCK, U.S. District Judge and author of *Disrobed*

EGO
IS THE
ENEMY

RYAN HOLIDAY

EGO
IS THE
ENEMY

PORTFOLIO

PENGUIN

PORTFOLIO / PENGUIN
An imprint of Penguin Random House LLC
375 Hudson Street
New York, New York 10014
penguin.com

ISBN 9781591847816 (hardcover)
ISBN 9780698192157 (ebook)

Printed in the United States of America
5 7 9 10 8 6 4

Do not believe that he who seeks to comfort you lives untroubled among the simple and quiet words that sometimes do you good. His life has much difficulty and sadness and remains far behind yours. Were it otherwise he would never have been able to find those words.

—RAINER MARIA RILKE

CONTENTS

PART II. SUCCESS

PART III. FAILURE

THE PAINFUL PROLOGUE

This is not a book about me. But since this is a book about ego, I'm going to address a question that I'd be a hypocrite not to have thought about.

Who the hell am I to write it?

My story is not particularly important for the lessons that follow, but I want to tell it briefly here at the beginning in order to provide some context. For I have experienced ego at each of its stages in my short life: Aspiration. Success. Failure. And back again and back again.

When I was nineteen years old, sensing some astounding and life-changing opportunities, I dropped out of college. Mentors vied for my attention, groomed me as their protégé. Seen as going places, I was *the kid*. Success came quickly.

After I became the youngest executive at a Beverly Hills talent management agency, I helped sign and work with a number of huge rock bands. I advised on books that went on to sell millions of copies and invent their own literary genres. Around the time I turned twenty-one, I came on as a strategist for American Apparel, then one of the hottest fashion brands in the world. Soon, I was the director of marketing.

By twenty-five, I had published my first book—which was an immediate and controversial best seller—with my face prominently on the cover. A studio optioned the rights to create a television show about my life. In the next few years, I accumulated many of the trappings of success—influence, a platform, press, resources, money, even a little notoriety. Later, I built a successful company on the back of those assets, where I worked with well-known, well-paying clients and did the kind of work that got me invited to speak at conferences and fancy events.

With success comes the temptation to tell oneself a story, to round off the edges, to cut out your lucky breaks and add a certain mythology to it all. You know, that arcing narrative of Herculean struggle for greatness against all odds: sleeping on the floor, being disowned by my parents, suffering for my ambition. It's a type of storytelling in which eventually your talent becomes your identity and your accomplishments become your worth.

But a story like this is never honest or helpful. In my retelling to you just now, I left a lot out. Conveniently omitted were the stresses and temptations; the stomach-turning drops and the mistakes—all the mistakes—were left on the cutting-room floor in favor of the highlight reel. They are the times I would rather not discuss: A public evisceration by someone I looked up to, which so crushed me at the time that I was later taken to the emergency room. The day I lost my nerve, walked into my boss's office, and told him I couldn't cut it and was going back to school—and meant it. The ephemeral nature of best-sellerdom, and how short it actually was (a week). The book signing that *one* person showed up at. The company I founded tearing itself to pieces and having to rebuild it. Twice. These are just some of the moments that get nicely edited out.

This fuller picture itself is still only a fraction of a life, but at least it hits more of the important notes—at least the important ones for this book: ambition, achievement, and adversity.

I'm not someone who believes in epiphanies. There is no one moment that changes a person. There are many. During a period of about six months in 2014, it seemed those moments were all happening in succession.

First, American Apparel—where I did much of my best work—teetered on the edge of bankruptcy, hundreds of millions of dollars in debt, a shell of its former self. Its founder, who I had deeply admired since I was a young man, was unceremoniously fired by his own handpicked board of directors, and down to sleeping on a friend's couch. Then the talent agency where I made my bones was in similar shape, sued peremptorily by clients to whom it owed a lot of money. Another mentor of mine seemingly unraveled around the same time, taking our relationship with him.

These were the people I had shaped my life around. The people I looked up to and trained under. Their stability—financially, emotionally, psychologically—was not just something I took for granted, it was central to my existence and self-worth. And yet, there they were, imploding right in front of me, one after another.

The wheels were coming off, or so it felt. To go from wanting to be like someone your whole life to realizing you *never* want to be like him is a kind of whiplash that you can't prepare for.

Nor was I exempt from this dissolution myself. Just when I could least afford it, problems I had neglected in my own life began to emerge.

Despite my successes, I found myself back in the city I started in, stressed and overworked, having handed much of my hard-earned freedom away because I couldn't say no to money and the thrill of a good crisis. I was wound so tight that the slightest disruption sent me into a sputtering, inconsolable rage. My work, which had always come easy, became labored. My faith in myself and other people collapsed. My quality of life did too.

I remember arriving at my house one day, after weeks on the road, and having an intense panic attack because the Wi-Fi wasn't working—*If I don't send these e-mails. If I don't send these e-mails. If I don't send these e-mails. If I don't send these e-mails* . . .

You think you're doing what you're supposed to. Society rewards you for it. But then you watch your future wife walk out the door because you aren't the person you used to be.

How does something like this happen? Can you really go from feeling like you're standing on the shoulders of giants one day, and then the next you're prying yourself out of the rubble of multiple implosions, trying to pick up the pieces from the ruins?

One benefit, however, was that it forced me to come to terms with the fact that I was a workaholic. Not in an "Oh, he just works too much" kind of way, or in the "Just relax and play it off" sense, but more, "If he doesn't start going to meetings and get clean, he will die an early death." I realized that the same drive and compulsion that had made me successful so early came with a price—as it had for so many others. It wasn't so much the amount of work but the outsized role it had taken in my sense of self. I was trapped so terribly inside my own head that I was a prisoner to my own thoughts. The result was a sort of treadmill of pain and frustration, and I needed to figure out why—unless I wanted to break in an equally tragic fashion.

For a long time, as a researcher and writer, I have studied history and business. Like anything that involves people, seen over a long enough timeline universal issues begin to emerge. These are the topics I had long been fascinated with. Foremost among them was ego.

I was not unfamiliar with ego and its effects. In fact, I had been researching this book for nearly a year before the events I have just recounted for you. But my painful experiences in this period brought the notions I was studying into focus in ways that I could never have previously understood.

It allowed me to see the ill effects of ego played out not just in myself, or across the pages of history, but in friends and clients and colleagues, some at the highest levels of many industries. Ego has cost the people I admire hundreds of millions of dollars, and like Sisyphus, rolled them back from their goals just as they've achieved them. I have now at least peeked over that precipice myself.

A few months after my own realization, I had the phrase "EGO IS THE ENEMY" tattooed on my right forearm. Where the words came from I don't know, probably from a book I read long, long ago, but they were immediately a source of great solace and direction. On my left arm, of similarly muddled attribution, it says: "THE OBSTACLE IS

THE WAY." It's these two phrases that I look at now, every single day, and use them to guide the decisions in my life. I can't help but see them when I swim, when I meditate, when I write, when I get out of the shower in the morning, and both prepare me—admonish me—to choose the right course in essentially any situation I might face.

I wrote this book not because I have attained some wisdom I feel qualified to preach, but because it's the book I wish existed at critical turning points in my own life. When I, like everyone else, was called to answer the most critical questions a person can ask themselves in life: Who do I want to be? And: What path will I take? (*Quod vitae sectabor iter.*)

And because I've found these questions to be timeless and universal, except for this note, I have tried to rely on philosophy and historical examples in this book instead of my personal life.

While the history books are filled with tales of obsessive, visionary geniuses who remade the world in their image with sheer, almost irrational force, I've found that if you go looking you'll find that history is also made by individuals who fought their egos at every turn, who eschewed the spotlight, and who put their higher goals above their desire for recognition. Engaging with and retelling these stories has been my method of learning and absorbing them.

Like my other books, this one is deeply influenced by Stoic philosophy and indeed all the great classical thinkers. I borrow heavily from them all in my writing just as I have leaned on them my entire life. If there is anything that helps you in this book, it will be because of them and not me.

The orator Demosthenes once said that virtue begins with understanding and is fulfilled by courage. We must begin by seeing ourselves and the world in a new way for the first time. Then we must fight to be different and fight to stay different—that's the hard part. I'm not saying you should repress or crush every ounce of ego in your life—or that doing so is even possible. These are just reminders, moral stories to encourage our better impulses.

In Aristotle's famous *Ethics*, he uses the analogy of a warped piece of wood to describe human nature. In order to eliminate warping or curvature, a skilled woodworker slowly applies pressure in the opposite direction—essentially, bending it straight. Of course, a couple of thousand years later Kant snorted, "Out of the crooked timber of humanity, nothing can be made straight." We might not ever be straight, but we can strive for *straighter*.

It's always nice to be made to feel special or empowered or inspired. But that's not the aim of this book. Instead, I have tried to arrange these pages so that you might end in the same place I did when I finished writing it: that is, you will think less of yourself. I hope you will be less invested in the story you tell about your own specialness, and as a result, you will be liberated to *accomplish* the world-changing work you've set out to achieve.

EGO
IS THE
ENEMY

INTRODUCTION

The first principle is that you must not fool yourself—
and you are the easiest person to fool.

—RICHARD FEYNMAN

Maybe you're young and brimming with ambition.
Maybe you're young and you're struggling. Maybe
you've made that first couple million, signed your
first deal, been selected to some elite group, or maybe you're
already accomplished enough to last a lifetime. Maybe
you're stunned to find out how empty it is at the top.
Maybe you're charged with leading others through a crisis.
Maybe you just got fired. Maybe you just hit rock bottom.

Wherever you are, whatever you're doing, your worst enemy
already lives inside you: your ego.

"Not me," you think. "No one would ever call me an egomaniac." Perhaps you've always thought of yourself as a pretty
balanced person. But for people with ambitions, talents, drives,
and potential to fulfill, ego comes with the territory. Precisely
what makes us so promising as thinkers, doers, creatives, and
entrepreneurs, what drives us to the top of those fields, makes
us vulnerable to this darker side of the psyche.

Now this is not a book about ego in the Freudian sense. Freud was fond of explaining the ego by way of analogy—our ego was the rider on a horse, with our unconscious drives representing the animal while the ego tried to direct them. Modern psychologists, on the other hand, use the word "egotist" to refer to someone dangerously focused on themselves and with disregard for anyone else. All these definitions are true enough but of little value outside a clinical setting.

The ego we see most commonly goes by a more casual definition: an unhealthy belief in our own importance. Arrogance. Self-centered ambition. That's the definition this book will use. It's that petulant child inside every person, the one that chooses getting his or her way over anything or anyone else. The need to be *better* than, *more* than, *recognized* for, far past any reasonable utility—that's ego. It's the sense of superiority and certainty that exceeds the bounds of confidence and talent.

It's when the notion of ourselves and the world grows so inflated that it begins to distort the reality that surrounds us. When, as the football coach Bill Walsh explained, "self-confidence becomes arrogance, assertiveness becomes obstinacy, and self-assurance becomes reckless abandon." This is the ego, as the writer Cyril Connolly warned, that "sucks us down like the law of gravity."

In this way, ego is the enemy of what you want and of what you have: Of mastering a craft. Of real creative insight. Of working well with others. Of building loyalty and support. Of longevity. Of repeating and retaining your success. It repulses advantages and opportunities. It's a magnet for enemies and errors. It is Scylla and Charybdis.

Most of us aren't "egomaniacs," but ego is there at the

root of almost every conceivable problem and obstacle, from why we can't win to why we need to win all the time and at the expense of others. From why we don't have what we want to why having what we want doesn't seem to make us feel any better.

We don't usually see it this way. We think something else is to blame for our problems (most often, other people). We are, as the poet Lucretius put it a few thousand years ago, the proverbial "sick man ignorant of the cause of his malady." Especially for successful people who can't see what ego prevents them from doing because all they can see is what they've already done.

With every ambition and goal we have—big or small— ego is there undermining us on the very journey we've put everything into pursuing.

The pioneering CEO Harold Geneen compared egoism to alcoholism: "The egotist does not stumble about, knocking things off his desk. He does not stammer or drool. No, instead, he becomes more and more arrogant, and some people, not knowing what is underneath such an attitude, mistake his arrogance for a sense of power and self-confidence." You could say they start to mistake that about themselves too, not realizing the disease they've contracted or that they're killing themselves with it.

If ego is the voice that tells us we're better than we really are, we can say ego inhibits true success by preventing a direct and honest connection to the world around us. One of the early members of Alcoholics Anonymous defined ego as "a conscious separation *from*." From what? Everything.

The ways this separation manifests itself negatively are

immense: We can't work with other people if we've put up walls. We can't improve the world if we don't understand it or ourselves. We can't take or receive feedback if we are incapable of or uninterested in hearing from outside sources. We can't recognize opportunities—or create them—if instead of seeing what is in front of us, we live inside our own fantasy. Without an *accurate* accounting of our own abilities compared to others, what we have is not confidence but delusion. How are we supposed to reach, motivate, or lead other people if we can't relate to their needs—because we've lost touch with our own?

The performance artist Marina Abramović puts it directly: "If you start believing in your greatness, it is the death of your creativity."

Just one thing keeps ego around—comfort. Pursuing great work—whether it is in sports or art or business—is often terrifying. Ego soothes that fear. It's a salve to that insecurity. Replacing the rational and aware parts of our psyche with bluster and self-absorption, ego tells us what we want to hear, when we want to hear it.

But it is a short-term fix with a long-term consequence.

EGO WAS ALWAYS THERE. NOW IT'S EMBOLDENED.

Now more than ever, our culture fans the flames of ego. It's never been easier to talk, to puff ourselves up. We can brag about our goals to millions of our fans and followers—things only rock stars and cult leaders used to have. We can follow and interact with our idols on Twitter, we can read books and sites and watch TED Talks, drink from a fire hose of inspiration and validation like never before (there's an app for that). We can name ourselves CEO of our exists-only-on-paper company. We can announce big news on social media and let the congratulations roll in. We can publish articles about ourselves in outlets that used to be sources of objective journalism.

Some of us do this more than others. But it's only a matter of degree.

Besides the changes in technology, we're told to believe in our uniqueness above all else. We're told to think big, live big, to be memorable and "dare greatly." We think that success requires a bold vision or some sweeping plan—after all, that's what the founders of this company or that championship team supposedly had. (But did they? Did they really?) We see risk-taking swagger and successful people in the media, and eager for our own successes, try to reverse engineer the right attitude, the right pose.

We intuit a causal relationship that isn't there. We assume the symptoms of success are the same as success itself—and in our naiveté, confuse the by-product with the cause.

Sure, ego has worked for some. Many of history's most famous men and women were notoriously egotistical. But so were many of its greatest failures. Far more of them, in fact. But here we are with a culture that urges us to roll the dice. To make the gamble, ignoring the stakes.

WHEREVER YOU ARE, EGO IS TOO.

At any given time in life, people find themselves at one of three stages. We're aspiring to something—trying to make a dent in the universe. We have achieved success—perhaps a little, perhaps a lot. Or we have failed—recently or continually. Most of us are in these stages in a fluid sense—we're aspiring until we succeed, we succeed until we fail or until we aspire to more, and after we fail we can begin to aspire or succeed again.

Ego is the enemy every step along this way. In a sense, ego is the enemy of building, of maintaining, and of recovering. When things come fast and easy, this might be fine. But in times of change, of difficulty . . .

And therefore, the three parts that this book is organized into: Aspire. Success. Failure.

The aim of that structure is simple: to help you suppress ego early before bad habits take hold, to replace the temptations of ego with humility and discipline when we experience success, and to cultivate strength and fortitude so that when fate turns against you, you're not wrecked by failure. In short, it will help us be:

- Humble in our aspirations
- Gracious in our success
- Resilient in our failures

This is not to say that you're not unique and that you don't have something amazing to contribute in your short time on this planet. This is not to say that there is not room to push past creative boundaries, to invent, to feel inspired, or to aim for truly ambitious change and innovation. On the contrary, in order to properly do these things and take these risks we need balance. As the Quaker William Penn observed, "Buildings that lie so exposed to the weather need a good foundation."

INTRODUCTION

SO, WHAT NOW?

This book you hold in your hands is written around one optimistic assumption: Your ego is not some power you're forced to satiate at every turn. It can be managed. It can be directed.

In this book, we'll look at individuals like William Tecumseh Sherman, Katharine Graham, Jackie Robinson, Eleanor Roosevelt, Bill Walsh, Benjamin Franklin, Belisarius, Angela Merkel, and George C. Marshall. Could they have accomplished what they accomplished—saving faltering companies, advancing the art of war, integrating baseball, revolutionizing football offense, standing up to tyranny, bravely bearing misfortune—if ego had left them ungrounded and self-absorbed? It was their sense of reality and awareness—one that the author and strategist Robert Greene once said we must take to like a spider in its web—that was at the core of their great art, great writing, great design, great business, great marketing, and great leadership.

What we find when we study these individuals is that they were grounded, circumspect, and unflinchingly real. Not that any of them were wholly without ego. But they knew how to suppress it, channel it, subsume it when it counted. They were great yet humble.

Wait, but so-and-so had a huge ego and was successful. But what about Steve Jobs? What about Kanye West?

We can seek to rationalize the worst behavior by pointing to outliers. But no one is truly successful *because* they are delusional, self-absorbed, or disconnected. Even if these traits are correlated or associated with certain well-known individuals, so are a few others: addiction, abuse (of themselves and

7

others), depression, mania. In fact, what we see when we study these people is that they did their best work in the moments when they fought back against these impulses, disorders, and flaws. Only when free of ego and baggage can anyone perform to their utmost.

For this reason, we're also going to look at individuals like Howard Hughes, the Persian king Xerxes, John DeLorean, Alexander the Great, and at the many cautionary tales of others who lost their grip on reality and in the process made it clear what a gamble ego can be. We'll look at the costly lessons they learned and the price they paid in misery and self-destruction. We'll look at how often even the most successful people vacillate between humility and ego and the problems this causes.

When we remove ego, we're left with what is real. What replaces ego is humility, yes—but rock-hard humility and confidence. Whereas ego is artificial, this type of confidence can hold weight. Ego is stolen. Confidence is earned. Ego is self-anointed, its swagger is artifice. One is girding yourself, the other gaslighting. It's the difference between potent and poisonous.

As you'll see in the pages that follow, that self-confidence took an unassuming and underestimated general and turned him into America's foremost warrior and strategist during the Civil War. Ego took a different general from the heights of power and influence after that same war and drove him to destitution and ignominy. One took a quiet, sober German scientist and made her not just a new kind of leader but a force for peace. The other took two different but equally brilliant and bold engineering minds of the twentieth century and built them up in a whirlwind of hype and celebrity before dashing their hopes against the rocks of failure, bankruptcy, scandal, and insanity. One guided one of the worst teams in NFL history to the Super Bowl in three seasons, and then on to be one of most dominant dynasties in the game. Meanwhile, countless other coaches, politicians, entrepreneurs, and writers have overcome similar odds—only to succumb to the more inevitable probability of handing the top spot right back to someone else.

Some learn humility. Some choose ego. Some are prepared for the vicissitudes of fate, both positive and negative. Others are not. Which will you choose? Who will you be?

You've picked up this book because you sense that you'll need to answer this question eventually, consciously or not.

Well, here we are. Let's get to it.

PART I

ASPIRE

Here, we are setting out to do something. We have a goal, a calling, a new beginning. Every great journey begins here—yet far too many of us never reach our intended destination. Ego more often than not is the culprit. We build ourselves up with fantastical stories, we pretend we have it all figured out, we let our star burn bright and hot only to fizzle out, and we have no idea why. These are symptoms of ego, for which humility and reality are the cure.

TO WHATEVER YOU ASPIRE,
EGO IS YOUR ENEMY . . .

> He is a bold surgeon, they say, whose hand does not
> tremble when he performs an operation upon his own
> person; and he is often equally bold who does not hesi-
> tate to pull off the mysterious veil of self-delusion, which
> covers from his view the deformities of his own conduct.
>
> —ADAM SMITH

Sometime around the year 374 B.C., Isocrates, one of the most well-known teachers and rhetoricians in Athens, wrote a letter to a young man named Demonicus. Isocrates had been a friend of the boy's recently deceased father and wanted to pass on to him some advice on how to follow his father's example.

The advice ranged from practical to moral—all communicated in what Isocrates described as "noble maxims." They were, as he put it, "precepts for the years to come."

Like many of us, Demonicus was ambitious, which is why Isocrates wrote him, because the path of ambition can be dangerous. Isocrates began by informing the young man that "no adornment so becomes you as modesty, justice, and self-control; for these are the virtues by which, as all men are agreed, the character of the young is held in restraint."

"Practice self-control," he said, warning Demonicus not to fall under the sway of "temper, pleasure, and pain." And "abhor flatterers as you would deceivers; for both, if trusted, injure those who trust them."

He wanted him to "Be affable in your relations with those who approach you, and never haughty; for the pride of the arrogant even slaves can hardly endure" and "Be slow in deliberation, but be prompt to carry out your resolves" and that the "best thing which we have in ourselves is good judgment." Constantly train your intellect, he told him, "for the greatest thing in the smallest compass is a sound mind in a human body."

Some of this advice might sound familiar. Because it made its way over the next two thousand years to William Shakespeare, who often warned about ego run amok. In fact, in *Hamlet*, using this very letter as his model, Shakespeare puts Isocrates' words in the mouth of his character Polonius in a speech to his son, Laertes. The speech, if you happen to have heard it, wraps up with this little verse.

This above all: to thine own self be true,
And it must follow, as the night the day,
Thou canst not then be false to any man.
Farewell. My blessing season this in thee!

As it happened, Shakespeare's words also made their way to a young United States military officer named William Tecumseh Sherman, who would go on to become perhaps this country's greatest general and strategic thinker. He may never have heard of Isocrates, but he loved the play and often quoted this very speech.

Like Demonicus', Sherman's father died when he was very young. Like Demonicus, he was taken under the wing of a wise, older man, in this case Thomas Ewing, a soon-to-be U.S. senator and friend of Sherman's father, who adopted the young boy and raised him as his own.

What's interesting about Sherman is that despite his connected father, almost no one would have predicted much more than regional accomplishments—least of all that he would one day need to take the unprecedented step of *refusing the presidency of the United States.* Unlike a Napoleon, who bursts upon the scene from nowhere and disappears in failure just as quickly, Sherman's ascent was a slow and gradual one.

He spent his early years at West Point, and then in the army. For his first few years in service, Sherman traversed nearly the entire United States on horseback, slowly learning with each posting. As the rumblings of Civil War broke out, Sherman made his way east to volunteer his services and he was shortly put to use at the Battle of Bull Run, a rather disastrous Union defeat. Benefiting from a dire shortage of leadership, Sherman was promoted to brigadier general and was summoned to meet with President Lincoln and his top military adviser. On several occasions, Sherman freely strategized and planned with the president, but at the end of his trip, he made one strange request; he'd accept his new promotion only with the assurance that he'd *not* have to assume superior command. Would Lincoln give him his word on that? With every other general asking for as much rank and power as possible, Lincoln happily agreed.

At this point in time, Sherman felt more comfortable as a

number two. He felt he had an honest appreciation for his own abilities and that this role best suited him. Imagine that—an ambitious person turning down a chance to advance in responsibilities because he actually wanted to be ready for them. Is that really so crazy?

Not that Sherman was always the perfect model of restraint and order. Early in the war, tasked with defending the state of Kentucky with insufficient troops, his mania and tendency to doubt himself combined in a wicked way. Ranting and raving about being undersupplied, unable to get out of his own head, paranoid about enemy movements, he broke form and spoke injudiciously to several newspaper reporters. In the ensuing controversy, he was temporarily recalled from his command. It took weeks of rest for him to recover. It was one of a few nearly catastrophic moments in his otherwise steadily ascendant career.

It was after this brief stumble—having learned from it—that Sherman truly made his mark. For instance, during the siege at Fort Donelson, Sherman technically held a senior rank to General Ulysses S. Grant. While the rest of Lincoln's generals fought amongst themselves for personal power and recognition, Sherman waived his rank, choosing to cheerfully support and reinforce Grant instead of issuing orders. This is your show, Sherman told him in a note accompanying a shipment of supplies; call upon me for any assistance I can provide. Together, they won one of the Union's first victories in the war.

Building on his successes, Sherman began to advocate for his famous march to the sea—a strategically bold and audacious plan, not born out of some creative genius but rather relying on the exact topography he had scouted and studied as a young officer in what had then seemed like a pointless backwater outpost.

Where Sherman had once been cautious, he was now confident. But unlike so many others who possess great ambition, he *earned* this opinion. As he carved a path from Chattanooga to Atlanta and then Atlanta to the sea, he avoided traditional battle after traditional battle. Any student of military history can see how the exact same invasion, driven by ego instead of a strong sense of purpose, would have had a far different ending.

His realism allowed him to see a path through the South that others thought impossible. His entire theory of maneuver warfare rested on deliberately avoiding frontal assaults or shows of strength in the form of pitched battles, and ignoring criticism designed to bait a reaction. He paid no notice and stuck to his plan.

By the end of the war, Sherman was one of the most famous men in America, and yet he sought no public office, had no taste for politics, and wished simply to do his job and then eventually retire. Dismissing the incessant praise and attention endemic to such success, he wrote as a warning to his friend Grant, "Be natural and yourself and this glittering flattery will be as the passing breeze of the sea on a warm summer day."

One of Sherman's biographers summarized the man and his unique accomplishments in a remarkable passage. It is why he serves as our model in this phase of our ascent.

> Among men who rise to fame and leadership two types are recognizable—those who are born with a belief in themselves and those in whom it is a slow growth dependent on actual achievement. To the

men of the last type their own success is a constant surprise, and its fruits the more delicious, yet to be tested cautiously with a haunting sense of doubt whether it is not all a dream. In that doubt lies true modesty, not the sham of insincere self-depreciation but the modesty of "moderation," in the Greek sense. It is poise, not pose.

One must ask: if your belief in yourself is *not* dependent on actual achievement, then what is it dependent on? The answer, too often when we are just setting out, is *nothing*. Ego. And this is why we so often see precipitous rises followed by calamitous falls.

So which type of person will you be?

Like all of us, Sherman had to balance talent and ambition and intensity, especially when he was young. His victory in this struggle was largely why he was able to manage the life-altering success that eventually came his way.

This probably all sounds strange. Where Isocrates and Shakespeare wished us to be self-contained, self-motivated, and ruled by principle, most of us have been trained to do the opposite. Our cultural values almost try to make us dependent on validation, entitled, and ruled by our emotions. For a generation, parents and teachers have focused on building up everyone's *self-esteem*. From there, the themes of our gurus and public figures have been almost exclusively aimed at inspiring, encouraging, and assuring us that we can do whatever we set our minds to.

In reality, this makes us weak. Yes, you, with all your talent and promise as a boy wonder or a girl-who's-going-places. We take it for granted that you have promise. It's why you've landed in the prestigious university you now attend, why you've secured the funding you have for your business, why you've been hired or promoted, why whatever opportunity you now have has fallen into your lap. As Irving Berlin put it, "Talent is only the starting point." The question is: Will you be able to make the most of it? Or will you be your own worst enemy? Will you snuff out the flame that is just getting going?

What we see in Sherman was a man deeply tied and connected to reality. He was a man who came from nothing and accomplished great things, without ever feeling that he was in someway *entitled* to the honors he received. In fact, he regularly and consistently deferred to others and was more than happy to contribute to a winning team, even if it meant less credit or fame for himself. It's sad to think that generations of young boys learned about Pickett's glorious cavalry charge, a Confederate charge that *failed,* but the model of Sherman as a quiet, unglamorous realist is forgotten, or worse, vilified.

One might say that the ability to evaluate one's own ability is the most important skill of all. Without it, improvement is impossible. And certainly ego makes it difficult every step of the way. It is certainly more pleasurable to focus on our talents and strengths, but where does that get us? Arrogance and self-absorption inhibit growth. So does fantasy and "vision."

In this phase, you must practice seeing yourself with a little distance, cultivating the ability to get out of your own head. Detachment is a sort of natural ego antidote. It's *easy* to be emotionally invested and infatuated with your own work. Any and every narcissist can do that. What is rare is not

EGO IS THE ENEMY

raw talent, skill, or even confidence, but humility, diligence, and self-awareness.

For your work to have truth in it, it must come from truth. If you want to be more than a flash in the pan, you must be prepared to focus on the long term.

We will learn that though we *think* big, we must act and live small in order to accomplish what we seek. Because we will be *action* and *education* focused, and forgo validation and status, our ambition will not be grandiose but iterative—one foot in front of the other, learning and growing and putting in the time.

With their aggression, intensity, self-absorption, and endless self-promotion, our competitors don't realize how they jeopardize their own efforts (to say nothing of their sanity). We will challenge the myth of the self-assured genius for whom doubt and introspection is foreign, as well as challenge the myth of pained, tortured artist who must sacrifice his health for his work. Where they are both divorced from reality and divorced from other people, we will be deeply connected, aware, and learning from all of it.

Facts are better than dreams, as Churchill put it.

Although we share with many others a *vision* for greatness, we understand that our *path* toward it is very different from theirs. Following Sherman and Isocrates, we understand that ego is our enemy on that journey, so that when we do achieve our success, it will not sink us but make us stronger.

TALK, TALK, TALK

Those who know do not speak.
Those who speak do not know.

—LAO TZU

In his famous 1934 campaign for the governorship of California, the author and activist Upton Sinclair took an unusual step. Before the election, he published a short book titled *I, Governor of California and How I Ended Poverty*, in which he outlined, in the past tense, the brilliant policies he had enacted as governor . . . the office he had not yet won.

It was an untraditional move from an untraditional campaign, intended to leverage Sinclair's best asset—as an author, he knew he could communicate with the public in a way that others couldn't. Now, Sinclair's campaign was always a long shot and hardly in good shape when they published the book. But observers at the time noticed immediately the effect it had—not on the voters, but on Sinclair himself. As Carey McWilliams later wrote about his friend's gubernatorial bid as it went south, "Upton not only realized that he would be defeated but seemed somehow to have lost interest in the campaign. In that vivid imagination of his, he had already acted out the part of 'I, Governor of California,' . . . so why bother to enact it in real life?"

The book was a best seller, the campaign a failure. Sinclair lost by something like a quarter of a million votes (a margin of more than 10 percentage points); he was utterly decimated in what was probably the first modern election. It's clear what happened: his talk got out ahead of his campaign and the will to bridge the gap collapsed. Most politicians don't write books like that, but they get ahead of themselves just the same.

It's a temptation that exists for everyone—for talk and hype to replace action.

The empty text box: "What's on your mind?" Facebook asks. "Compose a new tweet," Twitter beckons. Tumblr. LinkedIn. Our inbox, our iPhones, the comments section on the bottom of the article you just read.

Blank spaces, begging to be filled in with thoughts, with photos, with stories. With what we're *going* to do, with what things *should* or *could* be like, what we hope will happen. Technology, asking you, prodding you, soliciting *talk*.

Almost universally, the kind of performance we give on social media is *positive*. It's more "Let me tell you how well things are going. Look how great I am." It's rarely the truth: "I'm scared. I'm struggling. I don't know."

At the beginning of any path, we're excited and nervous. So we seek to comfort ourselves externally instead of inwardly. There's a weak side to each of us, that—like a trade union—isn't exactly malicious but at the end of the day still wants get as much public credit and attention as it can for doing the least. That side we call ego.

The writer and former Gawker blogger Emily Gould—a real-life Hannah Horvath if there ever was one—realized this during her two-year struggle to get a novel published. Though she had a six-figure book deal, she was stuck. Why? She was too busy "spending a lot of time on the Internet," that's why.

> In fact, I can't really remember anything else I did in 2010. I tumbld, I tweeted, and I scrolled. This didn't earn me any money but it felt like work. I justified my habits to myself in various ways. I was building my brand. Blogging was a creative act—even "curating" by reblogging someone else's post was a creative act, if you squinted. It was also the only creative thing I was doing.

In other words, she did what a lot of us do when we're scared or overwhelmed by a project: she did everything *but* focus on it. The actual novel she was supposed to be working on stalled completely. For a year.

It was easier to talk about writing, to do the exciting things related to art and creativity and literature, than to commit the act itself. She's not the only one. Someone recently published a book called *Working On My Novel*, filled with social media posts from writers who are clearly *not* working on their novels.

Writing, like so many creative acts, is hard. Sitting there, staring, mad at yourself, mad at the material because it doesn't seem good enough and *you* don't seem good enough.

In fact, many valuable endeavors we undertake are painfully difficult, whether it's coding a new startup or mastering a craft. But talking, talking is always easy.

We seem to think that silence is a sign of weakness. That being ignored is tantamount to death (and for the ego, this is true). So we talk, talk, talk as though our life depends on it.

In actuality, silence is strength—particularly early on in any journey. As the philosopher (and as it happens, a hater of newspapers and their chatter) Kierkegaard warned, "Mere gossip anticipates real talk, and to express what is still in thought weakens action by forestalling it."

And that's what is so insidious about *talk*. Anyone can talk about himself or herself. Even a child knows how to gossip and chatter. Most people are decent at hype and sales. So what is scarce and rare? Silence. The ability to deliberately keep yourself out of the conversation and subsist without its validation. Silence is the respite of the confident and the strong.

Sherman had a good rule he tried to observe. "Never give reasons for you what think or do until you must. Maybe, after a while, a better reason will pop into your head." The baseball and football great Bo Jackson decided he had two things he wanted to accomplish as an athlete at Auburn: he would win the Heisman Trophy and be taken first in the NFL draft. Do you know who he told? Nobody but his girlfriend.

Strategic flexibility is not the only benefit of silence while others chatter. It is also psychology. The poet Hesiod had this in mind when he said, "A man's best treasure is a thrifty tongue."

Talk depletes us. Talking and doing fight for the same

resources. Research shows that while goal visualization is important, after a certain point our mind begins to confuse it with actual progress. The same goes for verbalization. Even talking aloud to ourselves while we work through difficult problems has been shown to significantly decrease insight and breakthroughs. After spending so much time thinking, explaining, and talking about a task, we start to feel that we've gotten closer to achieving it. Or worse, when things get tough, we feel we can toss the whole project aside because we've given it our best try, although of course we haven't.

The more difficult the task, the more uncertain the outcome, the more costly talk will be and the farther we run from actual accountability. It's sapped us of the energy desperately needed to conquer what Steven Pressfield calls the "Resistance"—the hurdle that stands between us and creative expression. Success requires a full 100 percent of our effort, and talk flitters part of that effort away before we can use it.

A lot of us succumb to this temptation—particularly when we feel overwhelmed or stressed or have a lot of work to do. In our building phase, resistance will be a constant source of discomfort. Talking—listening to ourselves talk, performing for an audience—is almost like therapy. *I just spent four hours talking about this. Doesn't that count for something?* The answer is no.

Doing great work is a struggle. It's draining, it's demoralizing, it's frightening—not always, but it can feel that way when we're deep in the middle of it. We talk to fill the void and the uncertainty. "Void," Marlon Brando, a quiet actor if there ever was one, once said, "is terrifying to most people." It is almost as if we are assaulted by silence or confronted by it, particularly if we've allowed our ego to lie to us over the years. Which is so damaging for one reason: the greatest work and art comes from *wrestling* with the void, facing it instead of scrambling to make it go away. The question is, when faced with your particular challenge—whether it is researching in a new field, starting a business, producing a film, securing a mentor, advancing an important cause—do you seek the respite of talk or do you face the struggle head-on?

Think about it: a *voice of a generation* doesn't call itself that. In fact, when you think about it, you realize just how *little* these voices seem to talk. It's a song, it's a speech, it's a book—the volume of work may be light, but what's inside it is concentrated and impactful.

They work quietly in the corner. They turn their inner turmoil into product—and eventually to stillness. They ignore the impulse to seek recognition before they act. They don't talk much. Or mind the feeling that others, out there in public and enjoying the limelight, are somehow getting the better end of the deal. (They are not.) They're too busy working to do anything else. When they do talk—it's *earned*.

The only relationship between work and chatter is that one kills the other.

Let the others slap each other on the back while you're back in the lab or the gym or pounding the pavement. Plug that hole—that one, right in the middle of your face—that can drain you of your vital life force. Watch what happens. Watch how much better you get.

TO BE OR TO DO?

In this formative period, the soul is unsoiled by warfare
with the world. It lies, like a block of pure, uncut Parian
marble, ready to be fashioned into—what?

—ORISON SWETT MARDEN

One of the most influential strategists and practitioners in modern warfare is someone most people have never heard of. His name was John Boyd.

He was a truly great fighter pilot, but an even better teacher and thinker. After flying in Korea, he became the lead instructor at the elite Fighter Weapons School at Nellis Air Force Base. He was known as "Forty-Second Boyd"—meaning that he could defeat any opponent, from any position, in less than forty seconds. A few years later he was quietly summoned to the Pentagon, where his real work began.

In one sense, the fact that the average person might not have heard of John Boyd is not unexpected. He never published any books and he wrote only one academic paper. Only a few videos of him survive and he was rarely, if ever, quoted in the media. Despite nearly thirty years of impeccable service, Boyd wasn't promoted above the rank of colonel.

On the other hand, his theories transformed maneuver warfare in almost every branch of the armed forces, not just in his own lifetime but even more so after. The F-15 and F-16 fighter jets, which reinvented modern military aircraft, were his pet projects. His primary influence was as an adviser; through legendary briefings he taught and instructed nearly every major military thinker in a generation. His input on the war plans for Operation Desert Shield came in a series of direct meetings with the secretary of defense, not through public or official policy input. His primary means of effecting change was through the collection of pupils he mentored, protected, taught, and inspired.

There are no military bases named after him. No battleships. He retired assuming that he'd be forgotten, and without much more than a small apartment and a pension to his name. He almost certainly had more enemies than friends.

This unusual path—What if it were deliberate? What if it made him *more* influential? How crazy would that be?

In fact, Boyd was simply living the exact lesson he tried to teach each promising young acolyte who came under his wing, who he sensed had the potential to be something—to be something different. The rising stars he taught probably have a lot in common with us.

The speech Boyd gave to a protégé in 1973 makes this clear. Sensing what he knew to be a critical inflection point in the life of the young officer, Boyd called him in for a meeting. Like many high achievers, the soldier was insecure and impressionable. He wanted to be promoted, and he wanted to do well. He was a leaf that could be blown in any direction and Boyd knew it. So he heard a speech that day that Boyd would give again and again, until it became a tradition and a rite of passage for a generation of transformative military leaders.

"Tiger, one day you will come to a fork in the road," Boyd said to him. "And you're going to have to make a decision about which direction you want to go." Using his hands to illustrate, Boyd marked off these two directions. "If you go that way you can be somebody. You will have to make compromises and you will have to turn your back on your friends. But you will be a member of the club and you will get promoted and you will get good assignments." Then Boyd paused, to make the alternative clear. "Or," he said, "you can go that way and you can do something—something for your country and for your Air Force and for yourself. If you decide you want to do something, you may not get promoted and you may not get the good assignments and you certainly will not be a favorite of your superiors. But you won't have to compromise yourself. You will be true to your friends and to yourself. And your work might make a difference. To be somebody or to do something. In life there is often a roll call. That's when you will have to make a decision."

And then Boyd concluded with words that would guide that young man and many of his peers for the rest of their lives. "To be or to do? Which way will you go?"

Whatever we seek to do in life, reality soon intrudes on our youthful idealism. This reality comes in many names and forms: incentives, commitments, recognition, and politics. In every case, they can quickly redirect us from *doing* to *being*. From *earning* to *pretending*. Ego aids in that deception every step of the way. It's why Boyd wanted young people to see that if we are not careful, we can very easily find ourselves corrupted by the very occupation we wish to serve.

How do you prevent derailment? Well, often we fall in love with an *image* of what success looks like. In Boyd's world, the number of stars on your shoulder or the nature of your appointment or its location could easily be confused as a proxy for real accomplishment. For other people, it's their job title, the business school they went to, the number of assistants they have, the location of their parking space, the grants they earn, their access to the CEO, the size of their paycheck, or the number of fans they have.

Appearances are deceiving. *Having* authority is not the same as *being* an authority. *Having* the right and *being* right are not the same either. Being promoted doesn't necessarily mean you're doing good work and it doesn't mean you are worthy of promotion (they call it failing upward in such bureaucracies). *Impressing people is utterly different from being truly impressive.*

So who are you with? Which side will you choose? This is the roll call that life puts before us.

Boyd had another exercise. Visiting with or speaking to groups of Air Force officers, he'd write on the chalkboard in big letters the words: DUTY, HONOR, COUNTRY. Then he would cross those words out and replace them with three others: PRIDE, POWER, GREED. His point was that many of the systems and structures in the military—the ones that soldiers navigate in order to get ahead—can corrupt the very values they set out to serve. There's a quip from the historian Will Durant, that a nation is born stoic and dies epicurean. That's the sad truth Boyd was illustrating, how positive virtues turn sour.

How many times have we seen this played out in our own short lives—in sports, in relationships, or projects or people that we care deeply about? This is what the ego does. It crosses out what matters and replaces it with what doesn't.

A lot of people want to change the world, and it's good that they do. You want to be the best at what you do. Nobody *wants* to just be an empty suit. But in practical terms, which of the three words Boyd wrote on the chalkboard are going to get you there? Which are you practicing now? What's fueling you?

The choice that Boyd puts in front of us comes down to purpose. *What is your purpose? What are you here to do?* Because purpose helps you answer the question "To be or to do?" quite easily. If what matters is *you*—your reputation, your inclusion, your personal ease of life—your path is clear: Tell people what they want to hear. Seek attention over the quiet but important work. Say yes to promotions and generally follow the track that talented people take in the industry or field you've chosen. Pay your dues, check the boxes, put in your time, and leave things essentially as they are. Chase your fame, your salary, your title, and enjoy them as they come.

"A man is worked upon by what he works on," Frederick Douglass once said. He would know. He'd been a slave, and he saw what it did to everyone involved, including the *slaveholders* themselves. Once a free man, he saw that the choices people made, about their careers and their lives, had the same effect. What you choose to do with your time and what you choose to do for money works on you. The egocentric path requires, as Boyd knew, many compromises.

If your purpose is something larger than you—to accomplish something, to prove something to yourself—then suddenly everything becomes both easier and more difficult.

Easier in the sense that you know now what it is you need to do and what is important to you. The other "choices" wash away, as they aren't really choices at all. They're distractions. It's about the *doing*, not the recognition. Easier in the sense that you don't need to compromise. Harder because each opportunity—no matter how gratifying or rewarding—must be evaluated along strict guidelines: Does this help me do what I have set out to do? Does this *allow* me to do what I need to do? Am I being selfish or self*less*?

In this course, it is not "Who do I want to be in life?" but "What is it that I want to accomplish in life?" Setting aside selfish interest, it asks: What calling does it serve? What principles govern my choices? Do I want to be like everyone else or do I want to do something different?

In other words, it's harder because *everything* can seem like a compromise.

Although it's never too late, the earlier you ask yourself these questions the better.

Boyd undeniably changed and improved his field in a way that almost no other theorist has since Sun Tzu or von Clausewitz. He was known as Genghis John for the way he never let obstacles or opponents stop him from what he needed to do. His choices were not without their costs. He was also known as the ghetto colonel because of his frugal lifestyle. He died with a drawerful of thousands of dollars in uncashed expense checks from private contractors, which he equated with bribes. That he never advanced above colonel was not his doing; he was repeatedly held back for promotions. He was forgotten by history as a punishment for the work he did.

Think about this the next time you start to feel entitled,

the next time you conflate fame and the American Dream. Think about how you might measure up to a great man like that.

Think about this the next time you face that choice: Do I *need* this? Or is it really about ego? Are you ready to make the right decision? Or do the prizes still glitter off in the distance?

To be or to do—life is a constant roll call.

BECOME A STUDENT

Let No Man's Ghost Come Back to Say My Training Let
Me Down.

—SIGN IN THE NEW YORK FIRE DEPARTMENT
TRAINING ACADEMY

In April in the early 1980s, a single day became one guitarist's nightmare and became another's dream, and dream job. Without notice, members of the underground metal band Metallica assembled before a planned recording session in a decrepit warehouse in New York and informed their guitarist Dave Mustaine he was being thrown out of the group. With few words, they handed him a bus ticket back to San Francisco.

That same day, a decent young guitarist, Kirk Hammett, barely in his twenties and member of a band called Exodus, was given the job. Thrown right into a new life, he performed his first show with the band a few days later.

One would assume that this was the moment Hammett had been waiting for his whole life. Indeed it was. Though only known in small circles at the time, Metallica was a band that seemed destined to go places. Their music had already begun to push the boundaries of the genre of thrash metal, and cult stardom had already begun. Within a few short years, it would be one of the biggest bands in the world, eventually selling more than 100 million albums.

It was around this time that Kirk came to what must have been a humbling realization—that despite his years of playing and being invited to join Metallica, he wasn't as good as he'd like to be. At his home in San Francisco, he looked for a guitar teacher. In other words, despite joining his dream group and quite literally turning professional, Kirk insisted that he needed more instruction—that he was still a student. The teacher he sought out had a reputation for being a teacher's teacher, and for working with musical prodigies like Steve Vai.

Joe Satriani, the man Hammett chose as his instructor, would himself go on to become known as one of the best guitar players of all time and sell more than 10 million records of his unique, virtuosic music. Teaching out of a small music shop in Berkeley, Satriani's playing style made him an unusual choice for Hammett. That was the point—Kirk wanted to learn what he didn't know, to firm up his understanding of the fundamentals so that he might continue exploring this new genre of music he now had a chance to pursue.

Satriani makes it clear where Hammett was lacking—it wasn't talent, certainly. "The main thing with Kirk . . . was he was a really good guitar player when he walked in the door. He was already playing lead guitar . . . he was already shredding. He had a great right hand, he knew most of his chords, he just didn't learn how to play in an environment where he learned all the names and how to connect everything together."

That didn't mean that their sessions were some sort of fun study group. In fact, Satriani explained that what separated Hammett from the others was his willingness to endure the type of instruction they wouldn't. "He was a good student. Many of his friends and contemporaries would storm out complaining thinking I was too harsh a teacher."

Satriani's system was clear: that there would be weekly lessons, that these lessons must be learned, and if they weren't, that Hammett was wasting everyone's time and needn't bother to come back. So for the next two years Kirk did as Satriani required, returning every week for objective feedback, judgment, and drilling in technique and musical theory for the instrument he would soon be playing in front of thousands, then tens of thousands, and then literally hundreds of thousands of people. Even after that two-year study period, he would bring to Satriani licks and riffs he'd been working on with the band, and learned to pare down the instinct for *more*, and hone his ability to do more with fewer notes, and to focus on *feeling* those notes and expressing them accordingly. Each time, he improved as a player and as an artist.

The power of being a student is not just that it is an extended period of instruction, it also places the ego and ambition in someone else's hands. There is a sort of ego ceiling imposed—one knows that he is not better than the "master" he apprentices under. Not even close. You defer to them, you subsume yourself. You cannot fake or bullshit them. An education can't be "hacked"; there are no short-cuts besides *hacking it* every single day. If you don't, they drop you.

We don't like thinking that someone is better than us. Or

that we have a lot left to learn. We want to be done. We want to be ready. We're busy and overburdened. For this reason, updating your appraisal of your talents in a downward direction is one of the most difficult things to do in life— but it is almost always a component of mastery. The pretense of knowledge is our most dangerous vice, because it prevents us from getting any better. Studious self-assessment is the antidote.

The result, no matter what your musical tastes happen to be, was that Hammett became one of the great metal guitarists in the world, taking thrash metal from an underground movement into a thriving global musical genre. Not only that, but from those lessons, Satriani honed his own technique and became much better himself. Both the student and the teacher would go on to fill stadiums and remake the musical landscape.

The mixed martial arts pioneer and multi-title champion Frank Shamrock has a system he trains fighters in that he calls plus, minus, and equal. Each fighter, to become great, he said, needs to have someone better that they can learn from, someone lesser who they can teach, and someone equal that they can challenge themselves against.

The purpose of Shamrock's formula is simple: to get real and continuous feedback about what they know and what they don't know from every angle. It purges out the ego that puffs us up, the fear that makes us doubt ourselves, and any laziness that might make us want to coast. As Shamrock observed, "False ideas about yourself destroy you. For me, I always stay a student. That's what martial arts are about, and you have to use that humility as a tool. You put yourself beneath someone you trust." This begins by accepting that others know more than you and that you can benefit from their knowledge, and then seeking them out and knocking down the illusions you have about yourself.

The need for a student mind-set doesn't stop with fighting or music. A scientist must know the core principles of science and the discoveries occurring on the cutting edge. A philosopher must know deeply, and also know how little they know, as Socrates did. A writer must be versed in the canon—and read and be challenged by her contemporaries too. A historian must know ancient and modern history, as well as their specialty. Professional athletes have teams of coaches, and even powerful politicians have advisers and mentors.

Why? To become great and to stay great, they must all know what came before, what is going on now, and what comes next. They must internalize the fundamentals of their domain and what surrounds them, without ossifying or becoming stuck in time. They must be always learning. We must all become our own teachers, tutors, and critics.

Think about what Hammett could have done—what we might have done in his position were we to suddenly find ourselves a rock star, or a soon-to-be-rock star in our chosen field. The temptation is to think: I've made it. I've arrived. They tossed the other guy because he's not as good as I am. They chose me *because I have what it takes*. Had he done that, we'd probably have never heard of him or the band. There are, after all, plenty of forgotten metal groups from the 1980s.

A true student is like a sponge. Absorbing what goes on around him, filtering it, latching on to what he can hold. A student is self-critical and self-motivated, always trying to improve his understanding so that he can move on to the next topic, the next challenge. A real student is also his own teacher and his own critic. There is no room for ego there.

Take fighting as an example again, where self-awareness is particularly crucial because opponents are constantly looking to match strength against weakness. If a fighter is not capable of learning and practicing every day, if he is not relentlessly looking for areas of improvement, examining his own shortcomings, and finding new techniques to borrow from peers and opponents, he will be broken down and destroyed.

It is not all that different for the rest of us. Are we not fighting for or against something? Do you think you are the only one who hopes to achieve your goal? You can't possibly believe you're the only one reaching for that brass ring.

It tends to surprise people how humble aspiring greats seem to have been. *What do you mean they weren't aggressive, entitled, aware of their own greatness or their destiny?* The reality is that, though they were confident, the act of being an eternal student kept these men and women humble.

"It is impossible to learn that which one thinks one already knows," Epictetus says. *You can't learn if you think you already know.* You will not find the answers if you're too conceited and self-assured to ask the questions. You cannot get better if you're convinced you are the best.

The art of taking feedback is such a crucial skill in life, particularly harsh and critical feedback. We not only need to take this harsh feedback, but actively solicit it, labor to seek out the negative precisely when our friends and family and brain are telling us that we're doing great. The ego avoids such feedback at all costs, however. Who wants to remand themselves to remedial training? It thinks it already knows how and who we are—that is, it thinks we are spectacular, perfect, genius, truly innovative. It dislikes reality and prefers its own assessment.

Ego doesn't allow for proper incubation either. To become what we ultimately hope to become often takes long periods of obscurity, of sitting and wrestling with some topic or paradox. Humility is what keeps us there, concerned that we don't know enough and that we must continue to study. Ego rushes to the end, rationalizes that patience is for losers (wrongly seeing it as a weakness), and assumes that we're good enough to give our talents a go in the world.

As we sit down to proof our work, as we make our first elevator pitch, prepare to open our first shop, as we stare out into the dress rehearsal audience, ego is the enemy—giving us wicked feedback, disconnected from reality. It's defensive, precisely when we cannot afford to be defensive. It blocks us from improving by telling us that we don't need to improve. Then we wonder why we don't get the results we want, why others are better and why their success is more lasting.

Today, books are cheaper than ever. Courses are free. Access to teachers is no longer a barrier—technology has done away with that. There is no excuse for not getting your education, and because the information we have before us is so vast, there is no excuse for ever ending that process either.

Our teachers in life are not only those we pay, as Hammett paid Satriani. Nor are they necessarily part of some training dojo, like it is for Shamrock. Many of the best teachers are free. They volunteer because, like you, they once were young and had the same goals you do. Many don't even know they are teaching—they are simply exemplars, or even historical figures whose lessons survive in books and essays. But ego makes us so hardheaded and hostile to feedback that it drives them away or puts them beyond our reach.

It's why the old proverb says, "When student is ready, the teacher appears."

DON'T BE PASSIONATE

You seem to want that *vivida vis animi* which spurs and excites most young men to please, to shine, to excel. Without the desire and the pains necessary to be considerable, depend upon it, you never can be so.

—LORD CHESTERFIELD

Passion—it's all about passion. Find your passion. Live passionately. Inspire the world with your passion.

People go to Burning Man to find passion, to be around passion, to rekindle their passion. Same goes for TED and the now enormous SXSW and a thousand other events, retreats, and summits, all fueled by what they claim to be life's most important force.

Here's what those same people haven't told you: your passion may be the very thing holding you back from power or influence or accomplishment. Because just as often, we *fail* with—no, *because of*—passion.

Early on in her ascendant political career, a visitor once spoke of Eleanor Roosevelt's "passionate interest" in a piece of social legislation. The person had meant it as a compliment. But Eleanor's response is illustrative. "Yes," she did support the cause, she said. "But I hardly think the word 'passionate' applies to me."

As a genteel, accomplished, and patient woman born while the embers of the quiet Victorian virtues were still warm, Roosevelt was above passion. She had purpose. She had direction. She wasn't driven by passion, but by *reason*.

George W. Bush, Dick Cheney, and Donald Rumsfeld, on the other hand, were passionate about Iraq. Christopher McCandless was bursting with passion as he headed "into the wild." So was Robert Falcon Scott as he set out to explore the arctic, bitten as he was with "the Pole mania" (as were many climbers of the tragic 1996 Everest climb, momentarily struck with what psychologists now call "goalodicy"). The inventor and investors of the Segway believed they had a world-changing innovation on their hands and put everything into evangelizing it. That all of these talented, smart individuals were fervent believers in what they sought to do is without dispute. It's also clear that they were also unprepared and incapable of grasping the objections and real concerns of everyone else around them.

The same is true for countless entrepreneurs, authors, chefs, business owners, politicians, and designers that you've never heard of—and never will hear of, because they sunk their own ships before they'd hardly left the harbor. Like every other dilettante, they had passion and lacked something else.

To be clear, I'm not talking about *caring*. I'm talking about passion of a different sort—unbridled enthusiasm, our willingness to pounce on what's in front of us with the full measure of our zeal, the "bundle of energy" that our teachers and gurus have assured us is our most important asset. It is that burning, unquenchable desire to start or to achieve some vague, ambitious, and distant goal. This seemingly innocuous motivation is so far from the right track it hurts.

Remember, "zealot" is just a nice way to say "crazy person."

A young basketball player named Lewis Alcindor Jr., who won three national championships with John Wooden at UCLA, used one word to describe the style of his famous coach: "*dispassionate.*" As in *not* passionate. Wooden wasn't about rah-rah speeches or inspiration. He saw those extra emotions as a burden. Instead, his philosophy was about being in control and doing your job and never being "passion's slave." The player who learned that lesson from Wooden would later change his name to one you remember better: Kareem Abdul-Jabbar.

No one would describe Eleanor Roosevelt or John Wooden or his notoriously quiet player Kareem as apathetic. They wouldn't have said they were frenetic or zealous either. Roosevelt, one of the most powerful and influential female activists in history and certainly America's most important First Lady, was known primarily for her grace, her poise, and her sense of direction. Wooden won ten titles in twelve years, including seven in a row, because he developed a system for winning and worked with his players to follow it. Neither of them were driven by excitement, nor were they bodies in constant motion. Instead, it took them years to become the person they became known as. It was a process of accumulation.

In our endeavors, we will face complex problems, often in situations we've never faced before. Opportunities are not usually deep, virgin pools that require courage and boldness to dive into, but instead are obscured, dusted over, blocked by various forms of resistance. What is really called for in these circumstances is clarity, deliberateness, and methodological determination.

But too often, we proceed like this . . .

A flash of inspiration: I want to do the best and biggest _____ ever. Be the youngest _____. The only one to _____. The "firstest with the mostest."

The advice: Okay, well, here's what you'll need to do step-by-step to accomplish it.

The reality: We hear what we want to hear. We do what we feel like doing, and despite being incredibly busy and working very hard, we accomplish very little. Or worse, find ourselves in a mess we never anticipated.

Because we only seem to hear about the passion of successful people, we forget that failures shared the same trait. We don't conceive of the consequences until we look at their trajectory. With the Segway, the inventor and investors wrongly assumed a demand much greater than ever existed. With the run-up to the war in Iraq, its proponents ignored objections and negative feedback because they conflicted with what they so deeply needed to believe. The tragic end to the *Into the Wild* story is the result of youthful naiveté and a lack of preparation. With Robert Falcon Scott, it was overconfidence and zeal without consideration of the real dangers. We imagine Napoleon was brimming with passion as he contemplated the invasion of Russia and only finally became free of it as he limped home with a fraction of the men he'd so confidently left with. In many more examples we see the same mistakes: overinvesting, underinvesting, acting before someone is really ready, breaking things that required delicacy—not so much malice as the drunkenness of passion.

Passion typically masks a weakness. Its breathlessness and impetuousness and franticness are poor substitutes for discipline, for mastery, for strength and purpose and perseverance. You need to be able to spot this in others and in yourself, because while the origins of passion may be earnest and good, its effects are comical and then monstrous.

Passion is seen in those who can tell you in great detail who they intend to become and what their success will be like—they might even be able to tell you specifically when they intend to achieve it or describe to you legitimate and sincere worries they have about the burdens of such accomplishments. They can tell you all the things they're going to do, or have even begun, but they cannot show you their progress. Because there rarely is any.

How can someone be busy and not accomplish anything? Well, that's the passion paradox.

If the definition of insanity is trying the same thing over and over and expecting different results, then passion is a form of mental retardation—deliberately blunting our most critical cognitive functions. The waste is often appalling in retrospect; the best years of our life burned out like a pair of spinning tires against the asphalt.

Dogs, god bless them, are passionate. As numerous squirrels, birds, boxes, blankets, and toys can tell you, they do not accomplish most of what they set out to do. A dog has an advantage in all this: a graciously short short-term memory that keeps at bay the creeping sense of futility and impotence. Reality for us humans, on the other hand, has no reason to be sensitive to the illusions we operate under. Eventually it will intrude.

What humans require in our ascent is purpose and realism. Purpose, you could say, is like passion with boundaries. Realism is detachment and perspective.

When we are young, or when our cause is young, we feel so intensely—passion like our hormones runs strongest in youth—that it seems wrong to take it slow. This is just our impatience. This is our inability to see that burning ourselves out or blowing ourselves up isn't going to hurry the journey along.

Passion is *about*. (I am so passionate about _____.) Purpose is *to* and *for*. (I must do _____. I was put here to accomplish _____. I am willing to endure _____ for the sake of this.) Actually, purpose deemphasizes the *I*. Purpose is about pursuing something outside yourself as opposed to pleasuring yourself.

More than purpose, we also need realism. Where do we start? What do we do first? What do we do right now? How are we sure that what we're doing is moving us forward? What are we benchmarking ourselves against?

"Great passions are maladies without hope," as Goethe once said. Which is why a deliberate, purposeful person operates on a different level, beyond the sway or the sickness. They hire professionals and *use* them. They ask questions, they ask what could go wrong, they ask for examples. They plan for contingencies. Then they are off to the races. Usually they get started with small steps, complete them, and look for feedback on how the next set can be better. They lock in gains, and then get better as they go, often leveraging those gains to grow exponentially rather than arithmetically.

Is an iterative approach less exciting than manifestos, epiphanies, flying across the country to surprise someone, or sending four-thousand-word stream-of-consciousness e-mails in the middle of the night? Of course. Is it less glamorous and bold than going all in and maxing out your credit cards because you believe in yourself? Absolutely. Same goes for the spreadsheets, the meetings, the trips, the phone calls, software, tools, and internal systems—and every how-to article ever written about them and the routines of famous people. Passion is form over function. Purpose is function, function, function.

The critical work that you want to do will require your deliberation and consideration. Not passion. Not naïveté.

It'd be far better if you were intimidated by what lies ahead—humbled by its magnitude and determined to see it through regardless. Leave passion for the amateurs. Make it about what you feel you *must* do and say, not what you care about and wish to be. Remember Talleyrand's epigram for diplomats, "Surtout, pas trop de zèle" ("Above all, not too much zeal"). Then you will do great things. Then you will stop being your old, good-intentioned, but ineffective self.

FOLLOW THE CANVAS STRATEGY

Great men have almost always shown themselves as ready
to obey as they afterwards proved able to command.

—LORD MAHON

I n the Roman system of art and science, there existed a
concept for which we have only a partial analog. Successful businessmen, politicians, or rich playboys would sub-
sidize a number of writers, thinkers, artists, and performers.
More than just being paid to produce works of art, these
artists performed a number of tasks in exchange for protec-
tion, food, and gifts. One of the roles was that of an
anteambulo—literally meaning "one who clears the path." An
anteambulo proceeded in front of his patron anywhere they
traveled in Rome, making way, communicating messages,
and generally making the patron's life easier.

The famous epigrammist Martial fulfilled this role for
many years, serving for a time under the patron Mela, a
wealthy businessman and brother of the Stoic philosopher
and political adviser Seneca. Born without a rich family,
Martial also served under another businessman named

Petilius. As a young writer, he spent most of his day traveling from the home of one rich patron to another, providing services, paying his respects, and receiving small token payments and favors in return.

Here's the problem: like most of us with our internships and entry-level positions (or later on, publishers or bosses or clients), Martial absolutely hated every minute of it. He seemed to believe that this system somehow made him a slave. Aspiring to live like some country squire, like the patrons he serviced, Martial wanted money and an estate that was all his own. There, he dreamed, he could finally produce his works in peace and independence. As a result, his writing often drags with a hatred and bitterness about Rome's upper crust, from which he believed he was cruelly shunted aside.

For all his impotent rage, what Martial couldn't see was that it was his unique position as an outsider to society that gave him such fascinating insight into Roman culture that it survives to this day. Instead of being pained by such a system, what if he'd been able to come to terms with it? What if—gasp—he could have appreciated the opportunities it offered? Nope. It seemed to eat him up inside instead.

It's a common attitude that transcends generations and societies. The angry, unappreciated genius is forced to do stuff she doesn't like, for people she doesn't respect, as she makes her way in the world. *How dare they force me to grovel like this! The injustice! The waste!*

We see it in recent lawsuits in which interns sue their employers for pay. We see kids more willing to live at home with their parents than to submit to something they're "overqualified" to work for. We see it in an inability to meet anyone else on their terms, an unwillingness to take a step back in order to potentially take several steps forward. *I will not let them get one over on me. I'd rather we both have nothing instead.*

It's worth taking a look at the supposed indignities of "serving" someone else. Because in reality, not only is the apprentice model responsible for some of the greatest art in the history of the world—everyone from Michelangelo to Leonardo da Vinci to Benjamin Franklin has been forced to navigate such a system—but if you're going to be the big deal you think you are going to be, isn't this a rather trivial temporary imposition?

When someone gets his first job or joins a new organization, he's often given this advice: Make other people look good and you will do well. Keep your head down, they say, and serve your boss. Naturally, this is not what the kid who was chosen over all the other kids for the position wants to hear. It's not what a Harvard grad expects—after all, they got that degree precisely to avoid this supposed indignity.

Let's flip it around so it doesn't seem so demeaning: It's not about kissing ass. It's not about making someone *look* good. It's about providing the support so that others can *be* good. The better wording for the advice is this: Find canvases for other people to paint on. Be an *anteambulo*. Clear the path for the people above you and you will eventually create a path for yourself.

When you are just starting out, we can be sure of a few fundamental realities: 1) You're not nearly as good or as important as you think you are; 2) You have an attitude that needs to be readjusted; 3) Most of what you think you know or most of what you learned in books or in school is out of date or wrong.

There's one fabulous way to work all that out of your system: attach yourself to people and organizations who are already successful and subsume your identity into theirs and move both forward simultaneously. It's certainly more glamorous to pursue your own glory—though hardly as effective. Obeisance is the way forward.

That's the other effect of this attitude: it reduces your ego at a critical time in your career, letting you absorb everything you can without the obstructions that block others' vision and progress.

No one is endorsing sycophancy. Instead, it's about seeing what goes on from the inside, and looking for opportunities for someone *other than yourself.* Remember that *anteambulo* means clearing the path—finding the direction someone already intended to head and helping them pack, freeing them up to focus on their strengths. In fact, making things better rather than simply looking as if you are.

Many people know of Benjamin Franklin's famous pseudonymous letters written under names like Silence Dogwood. What a clever young prodigy, they think, and miss the most impressive part entirely: Franklin wrote those letters, submitted them by sliding them under the print-shop door, and received absolutely no credit for them until much later in his life. In fact, it was his brother, the owner, who profited from their immense popularity, regularly running them on the front page of his newspaper. Franklin was playing the long game, though—learning how public opinion worked, generating awareness of what he believed in, crafting his style and tone and wit. It was a strategy he used time and again over his career—once even publishing in his competitor's paper in order to undermine a third competitor—for

Franklin saw the constant benefit in making *other people* look good and letting them take credit for your ideas.

Bill Belichick, the four-time Super Bowl–winning head coach of the New England Patriots, made his way up the ranks of the NFL by loving and mastering the one part of the job that coaches disliked at the time: analyzing film. His first job in professional football, for the Baltimore Colts, was one he volunteered to take without pay—and his insights, which provided ammunition and critical strategies for the game, were attributed exclusively to the more senior coaches. He thrived on what was considered grunt work, asked for it and strove to become the best at precisely what others thought they were too good for. "He was like a sponge, taking it all in, listening to everything," one coach said. "You gave him an assignment and he disappeared into a room and you didn't see him again until it was done, and then he wanted to do more," said another. As you can guess, Belichick started getting paid very soon.

Before that, as a young high school player, he was so knowledgeable about the game that he functioned as a sort of assistant coach even while playing the game. Belichick's father, himself an assistant football coach for Navy, taught him a critical lesson in football politics: that if he wanted to give his coach feedback or question a decision, he needed to do it in private and self-effacingly so as not to offend his superior. He learned how to be a rising star without threatening or alienating anyone. In other words, he had mastered the canvas strategy.

You can see how easily entitlement and a sense of superiority (the trappings of ego) would have made the accomplishments of either of these men impossible. Franklin would never have been published if he'd prioritized credit over creative expression—indeed, when his brother found out, he literally beat him out of jealousy and anger. Belichick would have pissed off his coach and then probably been benched if he had one-upped him in public. He certainly wouldn't have taken his first job for free, and he wouldn't have sat through thousands of hours of film if he cared about status. Greatness comes from humble beginnings; it comes from grunt work. It means you're the least important person in the room—until you change that with results.

There is an old saying, "Say little, do much." What we really ought to do is update and apply a version of that to our early approach. Be *lesser*, do *more*. Imagine if for every person you met, you thought of some way to help them, something you could do for them? And you looked at it in a way that entirely benefited them and not you. The cumulative effect this would have over time would be profound: You'd learn a great deal by solving diverse problems. You'd develop a reputation for being indispensable. You'd have countless new relationships. You'd have an enormous bank of favors to call upon down the road.

That's what the canvas strategy is about—helping yourself by helping others. Making a concerted effort to trade your short-term gratification for a longer-term payoff. Whereas everyone else wants to get credit and be "respected," you can forget credit. You can forget it so hard that you're *glad* when others get it instead of you—that was your aim, after all. Let the others take their credit on credit, while you defer and earn interest on the principal.

The *strategy* part of it is the hardest. It's easy to be bitter, like Martial. To hate even the thought of subservience. To despise those who have more means, more experience, or more status than you. To tell yourself that every second not spent doing your work, or working on yourself, is a waste of your gift. To insist, *I will not be demeaned like this.*

Once we fight this emotional and egotistical impulse, the canvas strategy is easy. The iterations are endless.

- Maybe it's coming up with ideas to hand over to your boss.
- Find people, thinkers, up-and-comers to introduce them to each other. Cross wires to create new sparks.
- Find what nobody else wants to do and do it.
- Find inefficiencies and waste and redundancies. Identify leaks and patches to free up resources for new areas.
- Produce more than everyone else and give your ideas away

In other words, discover opportunities to promote their creativity, find outlets and people for collaboration, and eliminate distractions that hinder their progress and focus. It is a rewarding and infinitely scalable power strategy. Consider each one an investment in relationships and in your own development.

The canvas strategy is there for you at any time. There is no expiration date on it either. It's one of the few that age does not limit—on either side, young or old. You can start at any time—before you have a job, before you're hired and while you're doing something else, or if you're starting something new or find yourself inside an organization without strong allies or support. You may even find that there's no reason to ever stop doing it, even once you've graduated to heading your own projects. Let it become natural and permanent; let others apply it to you while you're too busy applying it to those above you.

Because if you pick up this mantle once, you'll see what most people's egos prevent them from appreciating: the person who clears the path ultimately controls its direction, just as the canvas shapes the painting.

RESTRAIN YOURSELF

I have observed that those who have accomplished the
greatest results are those who "keep under the body";
are those who never grow excited or lose self-control,
but are always calm, self-possessed, patient, and polite.

—BOOKER T. WASHINGTON

People who knew Jackie Robinson as a young man
probably wouldn't have predicted that they'd one
day see him become the first black player in Major
League Baseball. Not that he wasn't talented, or that the
idea of eventually integrating white baseball was inconceivable, it's that he wasn't exactly known for his restraint
and poise.

As a teenager, Robinson ran with a small gang of friends
who regularly found themselves in trouble with local police.
He challenged a fellow student to a fight at a junior college
picnic for using a slur. In a basketball game, he surreptitiously struck a hard-fouling white opponent with the ball
so forcefully that the kid bled everywhere. He was arrested
more than once for arguing with and challenging police,
who he felt treated him unfairly.

Before he started at UCLA, he spent the night in jail (and had a gun drawn on him by an officer) for nearly fighting a white man who'd insulted his friends. And in addition to rumors of inciting protests against racism, Jackie Robinson effectively ended his career as a military officer at Camp Hood in 1944 when a bus driver attempted to force him to sit in the back in spite of laws that forbade segregation on base buses. By arguing and cursing at the driver and then directly challenging his commanding officer after the fracas, Jackie set in motion a series of events that led to a court-martial. Despite being acquitted, he was discharged shortly afterward.

It's not just understandable and human that he did this; it was probably the right thing to do. Why should he let anyone else treat him that way? No one should have to stand for that.

Except sometimes they do. Are there not goals so important that we'd put up with anything to achieve them?

When Branch Rickey, the manager and owner of the Brooklyn Dodgers, scouted Jackie to potentially become the first black player in baseball, he had one question: Do you have the guts? "I'm looking," Rickey told him, "for a ball player with the guts *not* to fight back." In fact, in their famous meeting, Rickey playacted the abuse that Robinson was likely to experience if he accepted Rickey's challenge: a hotel clerk refusing him a room, a rude waiter in a restaurant, an opponent shouting slurs. This, Robinson assured him, he was ready to handle.

There were plenty of players Rickey could have gone with. But he needed one who wouldn't let his ego block him from seeing the bigger picture.

As he started in baseball's farm system, then in the pros, Robinson faced more than just slights from service staff or reticent players. There was an aggressive, coordinated campaign to libel, boo, provoke, freeze out, attack, maim, or even kill. In his career, he was hit by more than seventy-two pitches, nearly had his Achilles tendon taken out by players who aimed their spikes at him, and that says nothing of the calls he was cheated out of and the breaks of the game that didn't go his way. Yet Jackie Robinson held to his unwritten pact with Rickey, never giving into explosive anger—however deserved. In fact, in nine years in the league, he never hit another player with his fist.

Athletes seem spoiled and hotheaded to us today, but we have no concept of what the leagues were like then. In 1956, Ted Williams, one of the most revered and respected players in the history of the game, was once caught *spitting* at his fans. As a white player he could not only get away with this, he later told reporters, "I'm not a bit sorry for what I did. I was right and I'd spit again at the same people who booed me today . . . Nobody's going to stop me from spitting." For a black player, this sort of behavior would have been not only unthinkable but shortsighted beyond comprehension. Robinson had no such freedom—it would have ended not only his career, but set back his grand experiment for a generation.

Jackie's path called for him to put aside both his ego and in some respects his basic sense of fairness and rights as a human being. Early in his career, the manager of the Philadelphia Phillies, Ben Chapman, was particularly brutal in his taunting during a game. "They're waiting for you in the jungles, black boy!" he yelled over and over. "We don't want you here, nigger." Not only did Jackie *not* respond—despite, as he later wrote, wanting to "grab one of those white sons of bitches and smash his teeth in with my despised black fist"—a month later he agreed to take a friendly photo with Chapman to help save the man's job.

The thought of touching, posing with such an asshole, even sixty years removed, almost turns the stomach. Robinson called it one of the most difficult things he ever did, but he was willing to because it was part of a larger plan. He understood that certain forces were trying to bait him, to ruin him. Knowing what he wanted and needed to do in baseball, it was clear what he would have to tolerate in order do it. He shouldn't have had to, but he did.

Our own path, whatever we aspire to, will in some ways be defined by the amount of nonsense we are willing to deal with. Our humiliations will pale in comparison to Robinson's, but it will still be hard. It will still be tough to keep our self-control.

The fighter Bas Rutten sometimes writes the letter *R* on both his hands before fights—for the word *rustig*, which means "relax" in Dutch. Getting angry, getting emotional, losing restraint is a recipe for failure in the ring. You cannot, as John Steinbeck once wrote to his editor, "[lose] temper as a refuge from despair." Your ego will do you no favors here, whether you're struggling with a publisher, with critics, with enemies, or a capricious boss. It doesn't matter that they don't understand or that you know better. It's too early for that. It's too soon.

Oh, you went to *college*? That doesn't mean the world is yours by right. But it was *the Ivy League*? Well, people are still going to treat you poorly, and they will still yell at you. You have a million dollars or a wall full of awards? That doesn't mean anything in the new field you're trying to tackle.

It doesn't matter how talented you are, how great your connections are, how much money you have. When you want to do something—something big and important and meaningful—you will be subjected to treatment ranging from indifference to outright sabotage. Count on it.

In this scenario, ego is the absolute opposite of what is needed. Who can afford to be jerked around by impulses, or believe that you're god's gift to humanity, or too important to put up with anything you don't like?

Those who have subdued their ego understand that it doesn't degrade *you* when others treat you poorly; it degrades them.

Up ahead there will be: Slights. Dismissals. Little fuck yous. One-sided compromises. You'll get yelled at. You'll have to work behind the scenes to salvage what should have been easy. All this will make you angry. This will make you want to fight back. This will make you want to say: *I am better than this. I deserve more.*

Of course, you'll want to throw that in other people's faces. Worse, you'll want to get in other people's faces, people who don't *deserve* the respect, recognition, or rewards they are getting. In fact, those people will often get perks *instead* of you. When someone doesn't reckon you with the seriousness that you'd like, the impulse is to correct them. (As we all wish to say: *Do you know who I am?!*) You want to remind them of what they've forgotten; your ego screams for you to indulge it.

Instead, you must do nothing. Take it. Eat it until you're sick. Endure it. Quietly brush it off and work harder. Play the game. Ignore the noise; for the love of God, do not let it distract you. Restraint is a difficult skill but a critical one. You will often be tempted, you will probably even be overcome. No one is perfect with it, but try we must.

It is a timeless fact of life that the up-and-coming must endure the abuses of the entrenched. Robinson was *twenty-eight* when he started with the Dodgers, and he'd already paid plenty of dues in life as both a black man and a soldier. Still, he was forced to do it again. It's a sad fact of life that new talents are regularly missed, and even when recognized, often unappreciated. The reasons always vary, but it's a part of the journey.

But you're not able to change the system until *after* you've made it. In the meantime, you'll have to find some way to make it suit your purposes—even if those purposes are just extra time to develop properly, to learn from others on their dime, to build your base and establish yourself.

As Robinson succeeded, after he had proved himself as the Rookie of the Year and as an MVP, and as his spot on the Dodgers was certain, he began to more clearly assert himself and his boundaries as a player and as a man. Having carved out his space, he felt that he could argue with umpires, he could throw his shoulder if he needed to make a player back off or to send a message.

No matter how confident and famous Robinson became, he never spit on fans. He never did anything that undermined his legacy. A class act from opening day until the end, Jackie

Robinson was not without passion. He had a temper and frustrations like all of us do. But he learned early that the tightrope he walked would tolerate only restraint and had no forgiveness for ego.

Honestly, not many paths do.

GET OUT OF YOUR OWN HEAD

A person who thinks all the time has nothing to think about except thoughts, so he loses touch with reality and lives in a world of illusions.

—ALAN WATTS

It is Holden Caulfield, the self-absorbed boy walking the streets of Manhattan, struggling to adjust to the world. It is a young Arturo Bandini in Los Angeles, alienating every person he meets as he tries to become a famous writer. It is the blue blood Binx Bolling in 1950s uptown New Orleans, trying to escape the "everydayness" of life.

These fictional characters all had something in common: they couldn't get out of their own heads.

In J. D. Salinger's *The Catcher in the Rye*, Holden can't stay in school, is petrified of growing up, and wants desperately to away from it all. In John Fante's *Ask the Dust* (part of a series known as *The Bandini Quartet*), this young writer doesn't *experience* the life he is living, he sees it all "across a page in a typewriter," wondering if nearly every second of his life is a poem, a play, a story, a news article with him as its main character. In Walker Percy's *The Moviegoer*, his protagonist, Binx, is addicted to watching movies, preferring an idealized version of life on the screen to his own uncomfortable ennui.

It's always dangerous to psychologize a writer based on his work, but these are famously autobiographical novels. When we look at the writers' lives, the facts are clear: J. D. Salinger really did suffer from a sort of self-obsession and immaturity that made the world too much for him to bear, driving him from human contact and paralyzing his genius. John Fante struggled to reconcile his enormous ego and insecurity with relative obscurity for most of his career, eventually abandoning his novels for the golf course and Hollywood bars. Only near death, blind with diabetes, was he finally able to get serious again. *The Moviegoer*, Walker Percy's first book, came only after he'd conquered his almost teenage indolence and existential crisis, which lasted alarmingly into his forties.

How much better could these writers have been had they managed to get through these troubles earlier? How much easier would their lives have been? It's an urgent question they pushed onto their readers with their cautionary characters.

Because sadly, this trait, the inability to get out of one's head, is not restricted to fiction. Twenty-four hundred years ago, Plato spoke of the type of people who are guilty of "feasting on their own thoughts." It was apparently common enough even then to find people who "instead of finding out how something they desire might actually come about, [they] pass that over, so as to avoid tiring deliberations about what's possible. They assume that what they desire is available and proceed to arrange the rest, taking pleasure in thinking through everything they'll do when they have what they want, thereby making their lazy souls even lazier." Real people preferring to live in passionate fiction than in actual reality.

The Civil War general George McClellan is the perfect example of this archetype. He was chosen to command the Union forces because he checked all the boxes of what a great general should be: West Point grad, proven in battle, a student of history, of regal bearing, loved by his men.

Why did he turn out to be quite possibly the worst Union general, even in a crowded field of incompetent and self-absorbed leaders? Because he could never get out of his own head. He was in love with his vision of himself as the head of a grand army. He could prepare an army for battle like a professional, but when it came to *lead* one into battle, when the rubber needed to meet the road, troubles arose.

He became laughably convinced that the enemy was growing larger and larger (it wasn't—at one point he actually had a three-times *advantage*). He was convinced of constant threats and intrigues from his political allies (there weren't any). He was convinced that the only way to win the war was with the perfect plan and a single decisive campaign (he was wrong). He was so convinced of all of it that he froze and basically did nothing . . . for months at a time.

McClellan was constantly thinking *about himself* and how wonderful he was doing—congratulating himself for victories not yet won, and more often, horrible defeats he had saved the cause from. When anyone—including his superiors—questioned this comforting fiction, he reacted like a petulant, delusional, vainglorious, and selfish ass. By itself that's insufferable, but it meant another thing: his personality made it impossible to do what he needed to do most—win battles.

A historian who fought under McClellan at Antietam later summed it up: "His egotism is simply colossal—there is no other word for it." We tend to think that ego equals confidence, which is what we need to *be in charge*. In fact, it can have the opposite effect. In McClellan's case it deprived him of the ability to lead. It robbed him of the ability to think that he even needed to act.

The repeated opportunities he missed would be laughable were it not for the thousands and thousands of lives they cost. The situation was made worse by the fact that two pious, quiet Southerners—Lee and Stonewall Jackson—with a penchant for taking the initiative were able to embarrass him with inferior numbers and inferior resources. Which is what happens when leaders get stuck in their own heads. It can happen to us too.

The novelist Anne Lamott describes that ego story well. "If you are not careful," she warns young writers, "station KFKD (K-Fucked) will play in your head twenty-four hours a day, nonstop, in stereo."

> Out of the right speaker in your inner ear will come the endless stream of self-aggrandizement, the recitation of one's specialness, of how much more open and gifted and brilliant and knowing and misunderstood and humble one is. Out of the left speaker will be the rap songs of self-loathing, the lists of all the things one doesn't do well, of all the mistakes one has made today and over an entire lifetime, the doubt, the assertion that everything that one touches turns to

shit, that one doesn't do relationships well, that one is in every way a fraud, incapable of selfless love, that one had no talent or insight, and on and on and on.

Anyone—particularly the ambitious—can fall prey to this narration, good and bad. It is natural for any young, ambitious person (or simply someone whose ambition is young) to get excited and swept up by their thoughts and feelings. Especially in a world that tells us to keep and promote a "personal brand." We're required to tell stories in order to sell our work and our talents, and after enough time, forget where the line is that separates our fictions from reality.

Ultimately this disability will paralyze us. Or it will become a wall between us and the information we need to do our jobs—which is largely why McClellan continually fell for flawed intelligence reports he ought to have known were wrong. The idea that his task was relatively straightforward, that he just needed to get started, was almost too easy and too obvious to someone who had thought so much about it all.

He's not that different from the rest of us. We're all full of anxieties, doubts, impotence, pains, and sometimes a little tinge of crazy. We're like teenagers in this regard.

As the psychologist David Elkind has famously researched, adolescence is marked by a phenomenon known now as the "imaginary audience." Consider a thirteen-year-old so embarrassed that he misses a week of class, positive that the entire school is thinking and murmuring about some tiny incident that in truth hardly anyone noticed. Or a teenage girl who spends three hours in front of the mirror each morning, as if she's about to go on stage. They do this because they're convinced that their every move is being watched with rapt attention by the rest of the world.

Even as adults, we're susceptible to this fantasy during a harmless walk down the street. We plug in some headphones and all of a sudden there's a soundtrack. We flip up our jacket collar and consider briefly how cool we must look. We replay the successful meeting we're heading *toward* in our head. The crowds part as we pass. We're fearless warriors, on our way to the top.

It's the opening credits montage. It's a scene in a novel. It feels good—so much better than those feelings of doubt and fear and normalness—and so we stay stuck inside our heads instead of participating in the world around us.

That's ego, baby.

What successful people do is curb such flights of fancy. They ignore the temptations that might make them feel important or skew their perspective. General George C. Marshall—essentially the opposite of McClellan even though they briefly held the same position a few generations apart— refused to keep a diary during World War II despite the requests of historians and friends. He worried that it would turn his quiet, reflective time into a sort of performance and self-deception. That he might second-guess difficult decisions out of concern for his reputation and future readers and warp his thinking based on how they would look.

All of us are susceptible to these obsessions of the mind—whether we run a technology startup or are working our way up the ranks of the corporate hierarchy or have fallen madly in love. The more creative we are, the easier it is to lose the thread that guides us.

Our imagination—in many senses an asset—is dangerous

when it runs wild. We have to rein our perceptions in. Otherwise, lost in the excitement, how can we accurately predict the future or interpret events? How can we stay hungry and aware? How can we appreciate the present moment? How can we be creative within the realm of practicality?

Living clearly and presently takes courage. Don't live in the haze of the abstract, live with the tangible and real, even if—especially if—it's uncomfortable. Be part of what's going on around you. Feast on it, adjust for it.

There's no one to perform for. There is just work to be done and lessons to be learned, in all that is around us.

THE DANGER OF EARLY PRIDE

A proud man is always looking down on things and people; and, of course, as long as you are looking down, you cannot see something that is above you.

—C. S. LEWIS

At eighteen, a rather triumphant Benjamin Franklin returned to visit Boston, the city he'd run away from seven months before. Full of pride and self-satisfaction, he had a new suit, a watch, and a pocketful of coins that he spread out and showed to everyone he ran into—including his older brother, whom he particularly hoped to impress. All posturing by a boy who was not much more than an employee in a print shop in Philadelphia.

In a meeting with Cotton Mather, one of the town's most respected figures, and a former adversary, Franklin quickly illustrated just how ridiculously inflated his young ego had become. Chatting with Mather as they walked down a hallway, Mather suddenly admonished him, "Stoop! Stoop!" Too caught up in his performance, Franklin walked right into a low ceiling beam. Mather's response was perfect: "Let this be a caution to you not always to hold your head so high," he said wryly. "Stoop, young man, stoop—as you go through this world—and you'll miss many hard thumps."

Christians believe that pride is a sin because it is a lie—it convinces people that they are better than they are, that they are better than God made them. Pride leads to arrogance and then away from humility and connection with their fellow man.

You don't have to be Christian to see the wisdom in this. You need only to care about your career to understand that pride—even in real accomplishments—is a distraction and a deluder.

"Whom the gods wish to destroy," Cyril Connolly famously said, "they first call promising." Twenty-five hundred years before that, the elegiac poet Theognis wrote to his friend, "The first thing, Kurnos, which gods bestow on one they would annihilate, is pride." Yet we pick up this mantle on purpose!

Pride blunts the very instrument we need to own in order to succeed: our mind. Our ability to learn, to adapt, to be flexible, to build relationships, all of this is dulled by pride. Most dangerously, this tends to happen either early in life or in the process—when we're flushed with beginner's conceit. Only later do you realize that that bump on the head was the least of what was risked.

Pride takes a minor accomplishment and makes it feel like a major one. It smiles at our cleverness and genius, as though what we've exhibited was merely a hint of what ought to come. From the start, it drives a wedge between the possessor and reality, subtly and not so subtly changing her perceptions of what something is and what it isn't. It is these strong opinions, only loosely secured by fact or accomplishment, that send us careering toward delusion or worse.

Pride and ego say:

- I am an *entrepreneur* because I struck out on my own.
- I am going to *win* because I am currently in the lead.
- I am a *writer* because I published something.
- I am *rich* because I made some money.
- I am *special* because I was chosen.
- I am *important* because I think I should be.

At one time or another, we all indulge this sort of gratifying label making. Yet every culture seems to produce words of caution against it. Don't count your chickens before they hatch. Don't cook the sauce before catching the fish. The way to cook a rabbit is first to catch a rabbit. Game slaughtered by words cannot be skinned. Punching above your weight is how you get injured. Pride goeth before the fall.

Let's call that attitude what it is: fraud. If you're doing the work and putting in the time, you won't need to cheat, you won't need to overcompensate.

Pride is a masterful encroacher. John D. Rockefeller, as a young man, practiced a nightly conversation with himself. "Because you have got a start," he'd say aloud or write in his diary, "you think you are quite a merchant; look out or you will lose your head—go steady."

Early in his career, he'd had some success. He'd gotten a

good job. He was saving money. He had a few investments. Considering his father had been a drunken swindler, this was no small feat. Rockefeller was on the right track. Understandably, a sort of self-satisfaction with his accomplishments—and the trajectory he was heading in—began to seep in. In a moment of frustration, he once shouted at a bank officer who refused to lend him money, "Some day I'll be the richest man in the world!"

Let's count Rockefeller as maybe the only man in the world to say that and then go on to *become* the richest man in the world. But for every one of him, there are a dozen more delusional assholes who said the exact same thing and genuinely believed it, and then came nowhere close—in part because their pride worked against them, and made other people hate them too.

All of this was why Rockefeller knew he needed to rein himself in and to privately manage his ego. Night after night he asked himself, "Are you going to be a fool? Are you going to let this money puff you up?" (However small it was.) "Keep your eyes open," he admonished himself. "Don't lose your balance."

As he later reflected, "I had a horror of the danger of arrogance. What a pitiful thing it is when a man lets a little temporary success spoil him, warp his judgment, and he forgets what he is!" It creates a sort of myopic, onanistic obsession that warps perspective, reality, truth, and the world around us. The childlike little prince in Saint-Exupéry's famous story makes the same observation, lamenting that "vain men never hear anything but praise." That's exactly why we can't afford to have it as a translator.

Receive feedback, maintain hunger, and chart a proper course in life. Pride dulls these senses. Or in other cases, it tunes up other negative parts of ourselves: sensitivity, a persecution complex, the ability to make everything about *us*.

As the famous conqueror and warrior Genghis Khan groomed his sons and generals to succeed him later in life, he repeatedly warned them, "If you can't swallow your pride, you can't lead." He told them that pride would be harder to subdue than a wild lion. He liked the analogy of a mountain. He would say, "Even the tallest mountains have animals that, when they stand on it, are higher than the mountain."

We tend to be on guard against negativity, against the people who are discouraging us from pursuing our callings or doubting the visions we have for ourselves. This is certainly an obstacle to beware of, though dealing with it is rather simple. What we cultivate less is how to protect ourselves against the validation and gratification that will quickly come our way if we show promise. What we don't protect ourselves against are people and things that make us feel good—or rather, *too* good. We must prepare for pride and kill it early—or it will kill what we aspire to. We must be on guard against that wild self-confidence and self-obsession. "The first product of self-knowledge is humility," Flannery O'Connor once said. This is how we fight the ego, by really knowing ourselves.

The question to ask, when you feel pride, then, is this: What am I missing right now that a more humble person might see? What am I avoiding, or running from, with my bluster, franticness, and embellishments? It is far better to ask and answer these questions now, with the stakes still low, than it will be later.

It's worth saying: just because you are quiet doesn't mean that you are without pride. Privately thinking you're better than others is still pride. It's still dangerous. "That on which you so pride yourself will be your ruin," Montaigne had inscribed on the beam of his ceiling. It's a quote from the playwright Menander, and it ends with "you who think yourself to be someone."

We are still striving, and it is the strivers who should be our peers—not the proud and the accomplished. Without this understanding, pride takes our self-conception and puts it at odds with the reality of our station, which is that we still have so far to go, that there is still so much to be done.

After hitting his head and hearing from Mather, Franklin spent a lifetime battling against his pride, because he wanted to do much and understood that pride would made it much harder. Which is why, despite what would be dizzying accomplishments in any era—wealth, fame, power—Franklin never had to experience most of the "misfortunes brought upon people by their carrying their heads too high."

At the end, this isn't about deferring pride because you don't deserve it yet. It isn't "Don't boast about what hasn't happened yet." It is more directly "Don't boast." There's nothing in it for you.

WORK, WORK, WORK

> The best plan is only good intentions unless it *degenerates into work.*
>
> —PETER DRUCKER

The painter Edgar Degas, though best known for his beautiful Impressionist paintings of dancers, toyed briefly with poetry. As a brilliant and creative mind, the potential for great poems was all there—he could see beauty, he could find inspiration. Yet there are no great Degas poems. There is one famous conversation that might explain why. One day, Degas complained to his friend, the poet Stéphane Mallarmé, about his trouble writing. "I can't manage to say what I want, and yet I'm full of ideas." Mallarmé's response cuts to the bone. "It's not with ideas, my dear Degas, that one makes verse. It's with words."

Or rather, with *work.*

The distinction between a professional and a dilettante occurs right there—when you accept that having an idea is not enough; that you must work until you are able to recreate your experience effectively in words on the page. As the philosopher and writer Paul Valéry explained in 1938, "A poet's function . . . is not to experience the poetic state: that is a private affair. His function is to create it in others." That is, his job is to produce work.

To be both a craftsman and an artist. To cultivate a product of labor and industry instead of just a product of the mind. It's here where abstraction meets the road and the real, where we trade thinking and talking for working.

"You can't build a reputation on what you're *going* to do," was how Henry Ford put it. The sculptor Nina Holton hit the same note in psychologist Mihaly Csikszentmihalyi's land-mark study on creativity. "That germ of an idea," she told him, "does not make a sculpture which stands up. It just sits there. So the next stage, of course, is the hard work." The investor and serial entrepreneur Ben Horowitz put it more bluntly: "The hard thing isn't setting a big, hairy, audacious goal. The hard thing is laying people off when you miss the big goal. . . . The hard thing isn't dreaming big. The hard thing is waking up in the middle of the night in a cold sweat when the dream turns into a nightmare."

Sure, you get it. You know that all things require work and that work might be quite difficult. But do you *really* understand? Do you have any idea just how much work there is going to be? Not work until you get your big break, not work until you make a name for yourself, but work, work, work, forever and ever.

Is it ten thousand hours or twenty thousand hours to mastery? The answer is that it doesn't matter. There is no end zone. To think of a number is to live in a conditional future. We're simply talking about a lot of hours—that to get where we want to go isn't about brilliance, but continual effort. While that's not a terribly sexy idea, it should be an encouraging one. Because it means it's all within reach—for all of us, provided we have the constitution and humbleness to be patient and the fortitude to put in the work.

By this point, you probably understand why the ego would bristle at this idea. *Within reach?!* it complains. *That means you're saying I don't have it now.* Exactly right. You don't. No one does.

Our ego wants the ideas and the fact that we aspire to do something about them to be enough. Wants the hours we spend *planning* and attending conferences or chatting with impressed friends to count toward the tally that success seems to require. It wants to be paid well for its time and it wants to do the fun stuff—the stuff that gets attention, credit, or glory.

That's the reality. Where we decide to put our energy decides what we'll ultimately accomplish.

As a young man, Bill Clinton began a collection of note cards upon which he would write names and phone numbers of friends and acquaintances who might be of service when he eventually entered politics. Each night, before he ever had a reason to, he would flip through the box, make phone calls, write letters, or add notations about their interactions. Over the years, this collection grew—to ten thousand cards (before it was eventually digitized). It's what put him in the Oval Office and continues to return dividends.

Or think of Darwin, working for decades on his theory of evolution, refraining from publishing it because it wasn't yet perfect. Hardly anyone knew what he was working on. No one said, *Hey Charles, it's okay that you're taking so long, because what you're working on is just so important.* They didn't know. *He* couldn't have known. He just knew that it wasn't done yet, that it could be better, and that that was enough to keep him going.

So: Do we sit down, alone, and struggle with our work? Work that may or may not go anywhere, that may be discouraging or painful? Do we *love* work, making a living to do work, not the other way around? Do we *love* practice, the way great athletes do? Or do we chase short-term attention and validation—whether that's indulging in the endless search for *ideas* or simply the distraction of talk and chatter?

Fac, si facis. (Do it if you're going to do it.)

There is another apt Latin expression: *Materiam superabat opus.* (The workmanship was better than the material.) The material we've been given genetically, emotionally, financially, that's where we begin. We don't control that. We do control what we make of that material, and whether we squander it.

As a young basketball player, Bill Bradley would remind himself, "When you are not practicing, remember, someone somewhere is practicing, and when you meet him he will win." The Bible says something similar in its own way: "Blessed are those servants whom the master finds awake when he comes." You can lie to yourself, saying that you put in the time, or pretend that you're working, but eventually someone will show up. You'll be tested. And quite possibly, found out.

Since Bradley went on to be an All-American, a Rhodes Scholar, then a two-time champion with the New York Knicks and a U.S. senator, you get the sense that this sort of dedication will take you places.

So we must have it. Because there is no triumph without toil.

Wouldn't it be great if work was as simple as opening a vein and letting the genius pour out? Or if you could walk into that meeting and spit brilliance off the top of your head? You walk up to the canvas, hurl your paint at it, and modern art emerges, right? That is the fantasy—rather, that is the lie.

Back to another popular old trope: Fake it 'til you make it. It's no surprise that such an idea has found increasing relevance in our noxiously bullshit, Nerf world. When it is difficult to tell a real producer from an adept self-promoter, of course some people will roll the dice and manage to play the confidence game. Make it so you don't have to fake it— that's they key. Can you imagine a doctor trying to get by with anything less? Or a quarterback, or a bull rider? More to the point, would you want them to? So why would you try otherwise?

Every time you sit down to work, remind yourself: I am delaying gratification by doing this. I am passing the marshmallow test. I am earning what my ambition burns for. I am making an investment in myself instead of in my ego. Give yourself a little credit for this choice, but not so much, because you've got to get back to the task at hand: practicing, working, improving.

Work is finding yourself alone at the track when the weather kept everyone else indoors. Work is pushing through the pain and crappy first drafts and prototypes. It is ignoring whatever plaudits others are getting, and more importantly, ignoring whatever plaudits *you* may be getting. Because there is work to be done. Work doesn't *want* to be good. It is made so, despite the headwind.

There is another old expression: You know a workman by the chips they leave. It's true. To judge your progress properly, just take a look at the floor.

FOR EVERYTHING THAT COMES NEXT, EGO IS THE ENEMY . . .

'Tis a common proof,
That lowliness is young ambition's ladder.

—SHAKESPEARE

We know where we want to end up: success. We want to matter. Wealth and recognition and reputation are nice too. We want it all.

The problem is that we're not sure that humility can get us there. We are petrified, as the Reverend Dr. Sam Wells put it, that if we are humble, we will end up "subjugated, trodden on, embarrassed and irrelevant."

Midway through his career, if you'd asked our model Sherman how he felt, he probably would have described himself in almost exactly those terms. He had not made much money. He had won no great battles. He had not seen his name in lights or headlines. He might have, at that moment, before the Civil War, begun to question the path he'd chosen, and whether those who follow it finished last.

This is the thinking that creates the Faustian bargain that turns most clean ambition into shameless addiction. In the early stages, ego can be temporarily adaptive. Craziness can pass for audaciousness. Delusions can pass for confidence, ignorance for courage. But it's just kicking the costs down the road.

Because no one ever said, reflecting on the whole of someone's life, "Man, that monstrous ego sure was worth it."

The internal debate about confidence calls to mind a well-known concept from the radio pioneer Ira Glass, which could be called the Taste/Talent Gap.

> All of us who do creative work . . . we get into it because we have good taste. But it's like there's a gap, that for the first couple years that you're making stuff, what you're making isn't so good . . . It's really not that great. It's *trying* to be good, it has ambition to be good, but it's not quite that good. But your taste—the thing that got you into the game—your taste is still killer, and your taste is good enough that you can tell that what you're making is kind of a disappointment to you.

It is in precisely this gap that ego can seem comforting. Who wants to look at themselves and their work and find that it does not measure up? And so here we might bluster our way through. Cover up hard truths with sheer force of personality and drive and passion. *Or,* we can face our shortcomings honestly and put the time in. We can let this humble us, see clearly where we are talented and where we need to improve, and then put in the work to bridge that gap. And we can set upon positive habits that will last a lifetime.

If ego was tempting in Sherman's time, in this era, we

are like Lance Armstrong training for the 1999 Tour de France. We are Barry Bonds debating whether to walk into the BALCO clinic. We flirt with arrogance and deceit, and in the process grossly overstate the importance of winning at all costs. Everyone is juicing, the ego says to us, you should too. *There's no way to beat them without it,* we think.

Of course, what is truly ambitious is to face life and proceed with quiet confidence in spite of the distractions. Let others grasp at crutches. It will be a lonely fight to be real, to say "I'm not going to take the edge off." To say, "I am going to be myself, the best version of that self. I am in this for the long game, no matter how brutal it might be." To *do,* not *be.*

For Sherman, it was precisely his choice that prepared him for the time his country and history most needed him—and allowed him to navigate the massive responsibilities that shortly came his way. In this quiet crucible, he'd forged a personality that was ambitious but patient, innovative without being brash, brave without being dangerous. He was a *real* leader.

You have a chance to do this yourself. To play a different game, to be *utterly* audacious in your aims. Because what comes next is going to test you in ways that you cannot begin to understand. For ego is a wicked sister of success.

And you're about to experience what that means.

PART II

SUCCESS

Here we are at the top of a mountain we worked hard to climb—or at least the summit is in sight. Now we face new temptations and problems. We breathe thinner air in an unforgiving environment. Why is success so ephemeral? Ego shortens it. Whether a collapse is dramatic or a slow erosion, it's always possible and often unnecessary. We stop learning, we stop listening, and we lose our grasp on what matters. We become victims of ourselves and the competition. Sobriety, open-mindedness, organization, and purpose—these are the great stabilizers. They balance out the ego and pride that comes with achievement and recognition.

TO WHATEVER SUCCESS
YOU HAVE ACHIEVED,
EGO IS THE ENEMY . . .

Two different characters are presented to our emulation; the one, of proud ambition and ostentatious avidity. The other, of humble modesty and equitable justice. Two different models, two different pictures, are held out to us, according to which we may fashion our own character and behaviour; the one more gaudy and glittering in its colouring; the other more correct and more exquisitely beautiful in its outline.

—ADAM SMITH

A t a business meeting in January 1924, Howard Hughes Sr., the successful inventor and tool magnate, stood up, convulsed, and died from a sudden heart attack at the age of fifty-four. His son, a quiet, reserved, and sheltered boy of just eighteen, inherited three fourths of the private company, which held patents and leases critical to oil drilling, worth nearly $1 million. Various family members were bequeathed the remaining shares.

In a move of almost incomprehensible foresight, the young Hughes, whom many saw as a spoiled little boy, made the decision to buy out his relatives and control the entire company himself. Against their objections and still legally considered a minor, Hughes leveraged his personal assets and nearly all the company's funds to purchase the stock, and in doing so, consolidated ownership of a business that would create billions of dollars of cash profit over the next century.

It was a bold move for a young man with essentially zero experience in business. And it was with similar boldness that over his career he would create one of the most embarrassing, wasteful, and dishonest business track records in history. In retrospect, his years at the helm of the Hughes empire resemble a deranged crime spree more than a capitalistic enterprise.

One cannot argue whether Hughes was gifted, visionary, and brilliant. He just was. Literally a mechanical genius, he was also one of the best and bravest pilots in the pioneer days of aviation. And as a businessman and filmmaker he had the ability to predict wide, sweeping changes that came to transform not just the industries he was involved in, but America itself.

Yet, after filtering out his acumen from the legend, glamour, and self-promotion at which he was so adept, only one image remains: an egomaniac who evaporated *hundreds of millions* of dollars of his own wealth and met a miserable, pathetic end. Not by accident, not because he was beset by unforeseen circumstances or competition, but almost exclusively due to his own actions.

A quick rundown of his feats—if you can call them that—provides a stark perspective:

After purchasing control of his father's tool company from his family, Hughes abandoned it almost immediately except to repeatedly siphon off its cash. He left Houston and never stepped foot in the company's headquarters again. He moved to Los Angeles, where he decided to become a film producer and celebrity. Trading stocks from his bedside, he lost more than $8 million in the market leading up to the Depression. His most well-known movie, *Hell's Angels*, took three years to make, lost $1.5 million on a budget of $4.2 million, and nearly bankrupted the tool company in the process. Then, not having learned a lesson the first time, Hughes lost another $4 million on Chrysler stock in early 1930.

He then put all this aside to enter the aviation business, creating a defense contractor called the Hughes Aircraft Company. Despite some astounding personal achievements as an inventor, Hughes's company was a failure. His two contracts during World War II, worth $40 million, were massive failures at the expense of the American taxpayer and himself. The most notable, the *Spruce Goose*—which Hughes called the *Hercules* and which was one of the biggest planes ever made—took more than five years to develop, cost roughly $20 million, and flew just a single time for barely a mile, only 70 feet above the water. At his insistence and expense, it then sat in an air-conditioned hangar in Long Beach for decades at the cost of $1 million a year. Deciding to double down on the film business, Hughes purchased the movie studio RKO and produced losses of over $22 million (and went from two thousand employees to fewer than five hundred as he ran it into the ground over several years). Tiring of these businesses as he had of the tool company, he forsook defense contracting and handed it off to executives to run, where it slowly began to thrive . . . because of his absence.

It would make sense to stop here to avoid belaboring the

issue—but that would risk skipping Hughes's egregious tax fraud; the plane crashes and fatal car accidents; the millions he wasted on private investigators, lawyers, contracts for starlets he refused to let act, property he never lived in; the fact that the only thing that got him to behave responsibly was the threat of public exposure; the paranoia, racism, and bullying; the failed marriages; the drug addiction; and dozens of other ventures and businesses he mismanaged.

"That we have made a hero out of Howard Hughes," a young Joan Didion wrote, "tells us something interesting about ourselves." She's absolutely right. For Howard Hughes, despite his reputation, was quite possibly one of the worst businessmen of the twentieth century. Usually a bad businessman fails and ceases to be in business anymore, making it hard to see what truly caused his failures. But thanks to the steady chain of profits from his father's company, which he found too boring to interfere with, Hughes was able to stay afloat, allowing us to see the damage that his ego repeatedly wrought—to himself as a person, to the people around him, to what he wanted to accomplish.

There is a scene from Howard's slow descent into madness that bears illustrating. His biographers have him sitting naked in his favorite white chair, unwashed, unkempt, working around the clock to battle lawyers, investigations, investors, in an attempt to save his empire and to hide his shameful secrets. One minute he would dictate some irrational multipage memo about Kleenex, food preparation, or how employees should not speak to him directly, and then he would turn around and seize upon a genuinely brilliant strategy to outrun his creditors and enemies. It was as if, they observed, his mind and business were split in two parts. It was as if, they wrote, "IBM had deliberately established a pair of subsidiaries, one to produce computers and profits, another to manufacture Edsels and losses." If someone was looking for a flesh-and-blood metaphor for ego and destruction, it would be hard to do better than this image of a man working furiously with one hand toward a goal and with the other working equally hard to undermine it.

Howard Hughes, like all of us, was not completely crazy or completely sane. His ego, fueled and exacerbated by physical injuries (mostly from plane and car crashes for which he was at fault) and various addictions, led him into a darkness that we can scarcely comprehend. There were brief moments of lucidity when the sharp mind of Hughes broke through—times when he made some of his best moves—but as he progressed through life, these moments became increasingly rare. Eventually, ego killed Howard Hughes as much as the mania and trauma did—if they were ever separate to begin with.

You can only see this if you want to see it. It's more attractive and exciting to see the rebel billionaire, the eccentric, the world renown, and the fame, and think: *Oh, how I want that.* You do not. Howard Hughes, like so many wealthy people, died in an asylum of his own making. He felt little joy. He enjoyed almost nothing of what he had. Most importantly, he *wasted.* He wasted so much talent, so much bravery, and so much energy.

Without virtue and training, Aristotle observed, "it is hard to bear the results of good fortune suitably." We can learn from Hughes because he was so publicly and visibly unable to bear his birthright properly. His endless taste for the spotlight, no matter how unflattering, gives us an opportunity to see our own tendencies, our own struggles with success and luck, refracted back through his tumultuous life. His enormous ego and its destructive path through Hollywood, through the defense industry, through Wall Street, through the aviation industry give us a look inside someone who was repeatedly felled by impulses we all have.

Of course, he's far from the only person in history to follow such an arc. Will you follow his trajectory?

Sometimes ego is suppressed on the ascent. Sometimes an idea is so powerful or timing is so perfect (or one is born into wealth or power) that it can temporarily support or even compensate for a massive ego. As success arrives, like it does for a team that has just won a championship, ego begins to toy with our minds and weaken the will that made us win in the first place. We know that empires always fall, so we must think about why—and why they seem to always collapse from within.

Harold Geneen was the CEO who more or less invented the concept of the modern international conglomerate. Through a series of acquisitions, mergers, and takeovers (more than 350 in all), he took a small company called ITT from $1 million in revenues in 1959 to nearly $17 *billion* in 1977, the year he retired. Some claimed that Geneen himself was an egotist—in any case, he spoke candidly about the effects that ego had in his industry and warned executives against it.

"The worst disease which can afflict business executives

in their work is not, as popularly supposed, alcoholism; it's egotism," Geneen famously said. In the *Mad Men* era of corporate America, there was a major drinking problem, but ego has the same roots—insecurity, fear, a dislike for brutal objectivity. "Whether in middle management or top management, unbridled personal egotism blinds a man to the realities around him; more and more he comes to live in a world of his own imagination; and because he sincerely believes he can do no wrong, he becomes a menace to the men and women who have to work under his direction," he wrote in his memoirs.

Here we are having accomplished something. After we give ourselves proper credit, ego wants us to think, *I'm special. I'm better. The rules don't apply to me.*

"Man is pushed by drives," Viktor Frankl observed. "But he is pulled by values." Ruled by or *ruling*? Which are you? Without the right values, success is brief. If we wish to do more than flash, if we wish to last, then it is time to understand how to battle this new form of ego and what values and principles are required in order to beat it.

Success is intoxicating, yet to sustain it requires sobriety. We can't keep learning if we think we already know everything. We cannot buy into myths we make ourselves, or the noise and chatter of the outside world. We must understand that we are a small part of an interconnected universe. On top of all this, we have to build an organization and a system around what we do—one that is about the *work* and not about *us*.

The verdict on Hughes is in. Ego wrecked him. A similar judgment awaits us all at some point. Over the course of your own career, you will face the choices that he did—that all people do. Whether you built your empire from nothing or inherited it, whether your wealth is financial or merely a cultivated talent, entropy is seeking to destroy it as you read this.

Can you handle success? Or will it be the worst thing that ever happened to you?

ALWAYS STAY A STUDENT

Every man I meet is my master in some point, and in
that I learn of him.

—RALPH WALDO EMERSON

The legend of Genghis Khan has echoed through history: A barbarian conqueror, fueled by bloodlust, terrorizing the civilized world. We have him and his Mongol horde traveling across Asia and Europe, insatiable, stopping at nothing to plunder, rape, and kill not just the people who stood in their way, but the cultures they had built. Then, not unlike his nomadic band of warriors, this terrible cloud simply disappeared from history, because the Mongols built nothing that could last.

Like all reactionary, emotional assessments, this could not be more wrong. For not only was Genghis Khan one of the greatest military minds who ever lived, he was a perpetual student, whose stunning victories were often the result of his ability to absorb the best technologies, practices, and innovations of each new culture his empire touched.

In fact, if there is one theme in his reign and in the several *centuries* of dynastic rule that followed, it's this: appropriation.

Under Genghis Khan's direction, the Mongols were as ruthless about stealing and absorbing the best of each culture they encountered as they were about conquest itself. Though there were essentially no technological inventions, no beautiful buildings or even great Mongol art, with each battle and enemy, their culture learned and absorbed something new. Genghis Khan was not born a genius. Instead, as one biographer put it, his was "a persistent cycle of pragmatic learning, experimental adaptation, and constant revision driven by his uniquely disciplined and focused will."

He was the greatest conqueror the world ever knew because he was more open to learning than any other conqueror has ever been.

Khan's first powerful victories came from the reorganization of his military units, splitting his soldiers into groups of ten. This he stole from neighboring Turkic tribes, and unknowingly converted the Mongols to the decimal system. Soon enough, their expanding empire brought them into contact with another "technology" they'd never experienced before: walled cities. In the Tangut raids, Khan first learned the ins and outs of war against fortified cities and the strategies critical to laying siege, and quickly became an expert. Later, with help from Chinese engineers, he taught his soldiers how to build siege machines that could knock down city walls. In his campaigns against the Jurched, Khan learned the importance of winning hearts and minds. By working with the scholars and royal family of the lands he conquered, Khan was able to hold on to and manage these territories in ways that most empires could not. Afterward, in every country or city he held, Khan would call for the smartest astrologers, scribes, doctors, thinkers, and advisers—anyone who could aid his troops and their efforts. His troops traveled with interrogators and translators for precisely this purpose.

It was a habit that would survive his death. While the Mongols themselves seemed dedicated almost solely to the art of war, they put to good use every craftsman, merchant, scholar, entertainer, cook, and skilled worker they came in contact with. The Mongol Empire was remarkable for its religious freedoms, and most of all, for its love of ideas and convergence of cultures. It brought lemons to China for the first time, and Chinese noodles to the West. It spread Persian carpets, German mining technology, French metalworking, and Islam. The cannon, which revolutionized warfare, was said to be the resulting fusion of Chinese gunpowder, Muslim flamethrowers, and European metalwork. It was Mongol openness to learning and new ideas that brought them together.

As we first succeed, we will find ourselves in new situations, facing new problems. The freshly promoted soldier must learn the art of politics. The salesman, how to manage. The founder, how to delegate. The writer, how to edit others. The comedian, how to act. The chef turned restaurateur, how to run the other side of the house.

This is not a harmless conceit. The physicist John Wheeler, who helped develop the hydrogen bomb, once observed that "as our island of knowledge grows, so does the shore of our ignorance." In other words, each victory and advancement that made Khan smarter also bumped him against new situations he'd never encountered before. It takes a special kind of humility to grasp that you know less, even as you know and grasp more and more. It's remembering Socrates' wisdom lay in the fact that he knew that he knew next to nothing.

With accomplishment comes a growing pressure to pretend that we know more than we do. To pretend we already know everything. *Scientia infla* (knowledge puffs up). That's the worry and the risk—thinking that we're set and secure, when in reality understanding and mastery is a fluid, continual process.

The nine-time Grammy– and Pulitzer Prize–winning jazz musician Wynton Marsalis once advised a promising young musician on the mind-set required in the lifelong study of music: "Humility engenders learning because it beats back the arrogance that puts blinders on. It leaves you open for truths to reveal themselves. You don't stand in your own way. . . . Do you know how you can tell when someone is truly humble? I believe there's one simple test: because they consistently observe and listen, the humble improve. They don't assume, 'I know the way.'"

No matter what you've done up to this point, you better still be a student. If you're not still learning, you're already dying.

It is not enough only to be a student at the beginning. It is a position that one has to assume for life. Learn from *everyone* and *everything*. From the people you beat, and the people who beat you, from the people you dislike, even from your supposed enemies. At every step and every juncture in life, there is the opportunity to learn—and even if the lesson is purely remedial, we must not let ego block us from hearing it again.

Too often, convinced of our own intelligence, we stay in a comfort zone that ensures that we never feel stupid (and are never challenged to learn or reconsider what we know). It obscures from view various weaknesses in our understanding, until eventually it's too late to change course. This is where the silent toll is taken.

Each of us faces a threat as we pursue our craft. Like sirens on the rocks, ego sings a soothing, validating song—which can lead to a wreck. The second we let the ego tell us we have *graduated*, learning grinds to a halt. That's why Frank Shamrock said, "Always *stay* a student." As in, it never ends.

The solution is as straightforward as it is initially uncomfortable: Pick up a book on a topic you know next to nothing about. Put yourself in rooms where you're the least knowledgeable person. That uncomfortable feeling, that defensiveness that you feel when your most deeply held assumptions are challenged—what about subjecting yourself to it *deliberately*? Change your mind. Change your surroundings.

An amateur is defensive. The professional finds learning (and even, occasionally, being shown up) to be enjoyable; they like being challenged and humbled, and engage in education as an ongoing and endless process.

Most military cultures—and people in general—seek to impose values and control over what they encounter. What made the Mongols different was their ability to weigh each situation objectively, and if need be, swap out previous practices for new ones. All great businesses start this way, but then something happens. Take the theory of disruption, which posits that at some point in time, every industry will be disrupted by some trend or innovation that, despite all the resources in the world, the incumbent interests will be incapable of responding to. Why is this? Why can't businesses change and adapt?

A large part of it is because they lost the ability to learn. They stopped being students. The second this happens to you, your knowledge becomes fragile.

The great manager and business thinker Peter Drucker says that it's not enough simply to want to learn. As people progress, they must also understand *how* they learn and then set up processes to facilitate this continual education. Otherwise, we are dooming ourselves to a sort of self-imposed ignorance.

DON'T TELL YOURSELF A STORY

Myth becomes myth not in the living but in the retelling.

—DAVID MARANISS

S tarting in 1979, football coach and general manager Bill Walsh took the 49ers from being the worst team in football, and perhaps professional sports, to a Super Bowl victory, in just three years. It would have been tempting, as he hoisted the Lombardi Trophy over his head, to tell himself that the quickest turnaround in NFL history had been his plan all along. It would have been tempting decades later, when he assembled his memoirs, to assume that narrative as well.

It's a sexy story. That his takeover, his turnaround, and the transformation were assiduously scheduled. That it all happened exactly as he wanted—because he was just that good and that talented. No one would have faulted him if he said that.

Yet he refused to indulge in those fantasies. When people asked Walsh whether he had a timetable for winning the Super Bowl, do you know what his answer was? The answer was always *no*. Because when you take over a team that bad, such ambitions would have been utterly delusional.

The year before he arrived, the 49ers were 2 and 14. The organization was demoralized, broken, without draft picks, and fully ensconced in a culture of losing. His first season, they lost another fourteen games. He nearly resigned midway through his second year, because he wasn't sure he could do it. Yet, twenty-four months from taking over (and a little over a year from having almost quit), there he was, the Super Bowl champion "genius."

How did it happen? How was that not part of the "plan"?

The answer is that when Bill Walsh took control, he wasn't focused on winning per se. Instead, he implemented what he called his "Standard of Performance." That is: *What* should be done. *When. How.* At the most basic level and throughout the organization, Walsh had only one timetable, and it was all about instilling these standards.

He focused on seemingly trivial details: Players could not sit down on the practice field. Coaches had to wear a tie and tuck their shirts in. Everyone had to give maximum effort and commitment. Sportsmanship was essential. The locker room must be neat and clean. There would be no smoking, no fighting, no profanity. Quarterbacks were told where and how to hold the ball. Linemen were drilled on thirty separate critical drills. Passing routes were monitored and graded down to the *inch*. Practices were scheduled to the minute.

It would be a mistake to think this was about control. The Standard of Performance was about instilling excellence. These seemingly simple but exacting standards mattered more than some grand vision or power trip. In his eyes, if the players take care of the details, "the score takes care of itself." The winning would happen.

Walsh was strong and confident enough to know that these standards would eventually contribute to victory. He was also humble enough to know that *when* victory would happen was not something he could predict. That it happened faster than for any coach in history? Well, that was a fortuitous break of the game. It was not because of his grand vision. In fact, in his second season, a coach complained to the owner that Walsh was too caught up in minutiae and had no goals to win. Walsh fired that coach for tattling.

We want so desperately to believe that those who have great empires *set out* to build one. Why? So we can indulge in the pleasurable planning of ours. So we can take full credit for the good that happens and the riches and respect that come our way. Narrative is when you look back at an improbable or unlikely path to your success and say: I knew it all along. Instead of: I hoped. I worked. I got some good breaks. Or even: I thought this *could* happen. Of course you didn't really know all along—or if you did, it was more faith than knowledge. But who wants to remember all the times you doubted yourself?

Crafting stories out of past events is a very human impulse. It's also dangerous and untrue. Writing our own narrative leads to arrogance. It turns our life into a story— and turns us into caricatures—while we still have to live it. As the author Tobias Wolff writes in his novel *Old School*, these explanations and stories get "cobbled together later, more or less sincerely, and after the stories have been repeated they put on the badge of memory and block all other routes of exploration."

Bill Walsh understood that it was really the Standard of Performance—the deceptively small things—that was responsible for the team's transformation and victory. But that's too boring for newspaper headlines. It's why he ignored it when they called him "the Genius."

To accept the title and the story wouldn't be a harmless personal gratification. These narratives don't change the past, but they do have the power to negatively impact our future.

His players shortly proved the risks inherent in letting a story go to their heads. Like most of us, they wanted to believe that their unlikely victory occurred because they were special. In the two seasons after their first Super Bowl, the team failed terribly—partly due to the dangerous confidence that accompanies these kinds of victories—losing 12 of 22 games. This is what happens when you prematurely credit yourself with powers you don't yet have control of. This is what happens when you start to think about what your rapid achievements *say about you* and begin to slacken the effort and standards that initially fueled them.

Only when the team returned wholeheartedly to the Standard of Performance did they win again (three more Super Bowls and nine conference or division championships in a decade). Only when they stopped with the stories and focused on the task at hand did they begin to win like they had before.

Here's the other part: once you win, everyone is gunning for you. It's during your moment at the top that you can afford ego the least—because the stakes are so much higher, the margins for error are so much smaller. If anything, your ability to listen, to hear feedback, to improve and grow matter more now than ever before.

Facts are better than stories and image. The twentieth-century financier Bernard Baruch had a great line: "Don't try to buy at the bottom and sell at the top. This can't be done—except by liars." That is, people's claims about what they're doing in the market are rarely to be trusted. Jeff Bezos, the founder of Amazon, has talked about this temptation. He reminds himself that there was "no aha moment" for his billion-dollar behemoth, no matter what he might read in his own press clippings. The founding of a company, making money in the market, or the formation of an idea is messy. Reducing it to a narrative retroactively creates a clarity that never was and never will be there.

When we are aspiring we must resist the impulse to reverse engineer success from other people's stories. When we achieve our own, we must resist the desire to pretend that everything unfolded exactly as we'd planned. There was no grand narrative. You should remember—you were there when it happened.

A few years ago, one of the founders of Google gave a talk in which he said that the way he judges prospective companies and entrepreneurs is by asking them "if they're going to change the world." Which is fine, except that's not how Google started. (Larry Page and Sergey Brin were two Stanford PhDs working on their dissertations.) It's not how YouTube started. (Its founders weren't trying to reinvent TV; they were trying to share funny video clips.) It's not how most true wealth was created, in fact.

Investor Paul Graham (who invested in Airbnb, reddit, Dropbox, and others), working in the same city as Walsh a few decades later, explicitly warns startups against having bold, sweeping visions early on. Of course, as a capitalist, he wants to fund companies that massively disrupt industries and change the world—that's where the money is. He wants them to have "frighteningly ambitious" ideas, but explains, "The way to do really big things seems to be to start with deceptively small things." He's saying you don't make a frontal attack out of ego; instead, you start with a small bet and iteratively scale your ambitions as you go. His other famous piece of advice, "Keep your identity small," fits well here. Make it about the work and the principles behind it—not about a glorious vision that makes a good headline.

Napoleon had the words "To Destiny!" engraved on the wedding ring he gave his wife. Destiny was what he'd always believed in, it was how he justified his boldest, most ambitious ideas. It was also why he overreached time and time again, until his real destiny was divorce, exile, defeat, and infamy. A great destiny, Seneca reminds us, is great slavery.

There is a real danger in believing it when people use the word "genius"—and it's even more dangerous when we let hubris tell ourselves we are one. The same goes for any label that comes along with a career: are we suddenly a "filmmaker," "writer," "investor," "entrepreneur," or "executive" because we've accomplished one thing? These labels put you at odds not just with reality, but with the real strategy that made you successful in the first place. From that place, we might think that success in the future is just the natural next part of the story—when really it's rooted in work, creativity, persistence, and luck.

Certainly Google's alienation from its own roots (confusing vision and potential with *scientific and technological prowess*) will cause it to stumble soon enough. It fact, the public failures of projects like Google Glass and Google Plus might be evidence of it already. They're not alone. Too often, artists who think it was "inspiration" or "pain" that fueled their art and create an image around that—instead of hard work and sincere hustle—will eventually find themselves at the bottom of a bottle or on the wrong end of a needle.

The same goes for us, whatever we do. Instead of pretending that we are living some great story, we must remain focused on the execution—and on executing with excellence. We must shun the false crown and continue working on what got us here.

Because that's the only thing that will keep us here.

WHAT'S IMPORTANT TO YOU?

To know what you like is the beginning of wisdom and
of old age.

—ROBERT LOUIS STEVENSON

A t the end of the Civil War, Ulysses S. Grant and his
friend William Tecumseh Sherman were two of the
most respected and important men in America.
Essentially the dual architects of the Union's victory, a
grateful country, with a snap of its fingers, said: Whatever
you like, as long as you live, is yours.

With this freedom at their disposal, Sherman and Grant
took different paths. Sherman, whose track we followed earlier, abhorred politics and repeatedly declined entreaties to
run for office. "I have all the rank I want," he told them.
Having seemingly mastered his ego, he would later retire to
New York City, where he lived in what was, by all appearances, happiness and contentment.

Grant, who had expressed almost no prior interest in
politics, and, in fact, had succeeded as a general precisely
because he didn't know how to play politics, chose instead to
pursue the highest office in the land: the presidency. Elected

by a landslide, he then presided over one of the most corrupt, contentious, and least effective administrations in American history. A genuinely good and loyal individual, he was not cut out for the dirty world of Washington, and it made quick work of him. He left office a maligned and controversial figure after two exhausting terms, almost surprised by how poorly it had gone.

After the presidency, Grant invested almost every penny he had to create a financial brokerage house with a controversial investor named Ferdinand Ward. Ward, a Bernie Madoff of his day, turned it into a Ponzi scheme, and publicly bankrupted Grant. As Sherman wrote with sympathy and understanding of his friend, Grant had "aimed to rival the millionaires, who would have given their all to have won any of his battles." Grant had accomplished so much, but to him, it wasn't enough. He couldn't decide what was important—what actually mattered—to him.

That's how it seems to go: we're never happy with what *we* have, we want what others have too. We want to have *more* than everyone else. We start out knowing what is important to us, but once we've achieved it, we lose sight of our priorities. Ego sways us, and can ruin us.

Compelled by his sense of honor to cover the debts of the firm, Grant took out a loan using his priceless war mementos as collateral. Broken in mind, spirit, and body, the last years of his life found him battling painful throat cancer, and racing to finish his memoirs so that he might leave his family with something to live on. He made it, just barely.

One shudders to think of the vital forces drained from this hero, who died at just sixty-three in agony and defeat, this straightforward, honest man who just couldn't help himself, who couldn't manage to focus, and ended up far outside the bounds of his ample genius. What could he have done with those years instead? How might have America looked otherwise? How much more could he have done and accomplished?

Not that he is unique in this regard. All of us regularly say yes unthinkingly, or out of vague attraction, or out of greed or vanity. Because we can't say no—because we might miss out on something if we did. We think "yes" will let us accomplish more, when in reality it prevents exactly what we seek. All of us waste precious life doing things we don't like, to prove ourselves to people we don't respect, and to get things we don't want.

Why do we do this? Well, it should be obvious by now.

Ego leads to envy and it rots the bones of people big and small. Ego undermines greatness by deluding its holder.

Most of us begin with a clear idea of what we want in life. We know what's important to us. The success we achieve, especially if it comes early or in abundance, puts us in an unusual place. Because now, all of a sudden, we're in a new place and have trouble keeping our bearings.

The farther you travel down that path of accomplishment, whatever it may be, the more often you meet other successful people who make you feel insignificant. It doesn't matter how well you're doing; your ego and their accomplishments make you feel like *nothing*—just as others make them feel the same way. It's a cycle that goes on ad infinitum . . . while our brief time on earth—or the small window of opportunity we have here—does not.

So we unconsciously pick up the pace to keep up with

others. But what if different people are running for different reasons? What if there is more than one race going on?

That's what Sherman was saying about Grant. There is a certain "Gift of the Magi" irony in how badly we chase what will not be truly pleasurable. At the very least, it won't last. If only we could all stop for a second.

Let's be clear: competitiveness is an important force in life. It's what drives the market and is behind some of mankind's most impressive accomplishments. On an individual level, however, it's absolutely critical that you know *who* you're competing with and *why*, that you have a clear sense of the space you're in.

Only you know the race you're running. That is, unless your ego decides the only way you have value is if you're *better* than, *have more* than, *everyone everywhere*. More urgently, each one of us has a unique potential and purpose; that means that we're the only ones who can evaluate and set the terms of our lives. Far too often, we look at other people and make their approval the standard we feel compelled to meet, and as a result, squander our very potential and purpose.

According to Seneca, the Greek word *euthymia* is one we should think of often: it is the sense of our own path and how to stay on it without getting distracted by all the others that intersect it. In other words, it's not about beating the other guy. It's not about having more than the others. It's about being what you are, and being as good as possible at it, without succumbing to all the things that draw you away from it. It's about going where you set out to go. About accomplishing the most that you're capable of in what you choose. That's it. No more and no less. (By the way, *euthymia* means "tranquillity" in English.)

It's time to sit down and think about what's truly important to you and then take steps to forsake the rest. Without this, success will not be pleasurable, or nearly as complete as it could be. Or worse, it won't last.

This is especially true with money. If you don't know how much you need, the default easily becomes: more. And so without thinking, critical energy is diverted from a person's calling and toward filling a bank account. When "you combine insecurity and ambition," the plagiarist and disgraced journalist Jonah Lehrer said when reflecting back on his fall, "you get an inability to say no to things."

Ego rejects trade-offs. Why compromise? Ego wants it *all*.

Ego tells you to cheat, though you love your spouse. Because you want what you have *and* what you don't have. Ego says that sure, even though you're just starting to get the hang of one thing, why not jump right in the middle of another? Eventually, you say yes to too much, to something too far beyond the pale. We're like Captain Ahab, chasing Moby Dick, for reasons we don't even understand anymore.

Maybe your priority actually is money. Or maybe it's family. Maybe it's influence or change. Maybe it's building an organization that lasts, or serves a purpose. All of these are perfectly fine motivations. But you do need to know. You need to know what you don't want and what your choices preclude. Because strategies are often mutually exclusive. One cannot be an opera singer *and* a teen pop idol at the same time. Life requires those trade-offs, but ego can't allow it.

So why do you do what you do? That's the question you need to answer. Stare at it until you can. Only then will you understand what matters and what doesn't. Only then can you say no, can you opt out of stupid races that don't matter, or even exist. Only then is it easy to ignore "successful" people, because most of the time they aren't—at least relative to you, and often even to themselves. Only then can you develop that quiet confidence Seneca talked about.

The more you have and do, the harder maintaining fidelity to your purpose will be, but the more critically you will need to. Everyone buys into the myth that *if only they had that*—usually what someone else has—they would be happy. It may take getting burned a few times to realize the emptiness of this illusion. We all occasionally find ourselves in the middle of some project or obligation and can't understand why we're there. It will take courage and faith to stop yourself.

Find out why you're after what you're after. Ignore those who mess with your pace. Let them covet what you have, not the other way around. Because that's independence.

ENTITLEMENT, CONTROL, AND PARANOIA

> One of the symptoms of approaching nervous break-
> down is the belief that one's work is terribly important.
>
> —BERTRAND RUSSELL

When Xerxes, the Persian emperor, crossed the Hellespont during his invasion of Greece, the waters surged up and destroyed the bridges his engineers had spent days building. And so he threw chains into the river, ordered it be given three hundred lashes, and branded it with hot irons. As his men delivered his punishment, they were ordered to harangue it: "You salt and bitter stream, your master lays this punishment upon you for injuring him, who never injured you." Oh, and he cut off the heads of the men who had built the bridges.

Herodotus, the great historian, called the display "presumptuous," which is probably an understatement. Surely "preposterous" and "delusional" are more appropriate. Then again, it was part of his personality. Shortly before this, Xerxes had written a letter to a nearby mountain in which he needed to cut a canal. You may be tall and proud, he wrote, but don't you dare cause me any trouble. Otherwise, I'll topple you into the sea.

How hilarious is that? More important, how pathetic?

Xerxes' delusional threats are unfortunately not a historical anomaly. With success, particularly power, come some of the greatest and most dangerous delusions: entitlement, control, and paranoia.

Hopefully you won't find yourself so crazed that you start anthropomorphizing, and inflicting retribution on inanimate objects. That's pure, recognizable crazy, and thankfully rare. What's more likely, and more common, is we begin to overestimate our own power. Then we lose perspective. Eventually, we can end like Xerxes, a monstrous joke.

"The Strongest Poison ever known," the poet William Blake wrote, "came from Caesar's Laurel Crown." Success casts a spell over us.

The problem lies in the path that got us to success in the first place. What we've accomplished often required feats of raw power and force of will. Both entrepreneurship and art required the creation of something where nothing existed before. Wealth means beating the market and the odds. Athletic champions have proved their physical superiority over opponents.

Achieving success involved ignoring the doubts and reservations of the people around us. It meant rejecting rejection. It required taking certain risks. We could have given up at any time, but we're here precisely because we didn't. Persistence and courage in the face of ridiculous odds are partially irrational traits—in some cases *really* irrational. When it works, those tendencies can feel like they've been vindicated.

And why shouldn't they? It's human to think that since it's been done once—that the world was changed in some big or small way—that there is now a magical power in our possession. We're here because we're bigger, stronger, smarter. That we *make* the reality we inhabit.

Right before he destroyed his own billion-dollar company, Ty Warner, creator of Beanie Babies, overrode the cautious objections of one of his employees and bragged, "I could put the Ty heart on manure and they'd buy it!" He was wrong. And the company not only catastrophically failed, he later narrowly missed going to jail.

It doesn't matter if you're a billionaire, a millionaire, or just a kid who snagged a good job early. The complete and utter sense of certainty that got you here can become a liability if you're not careful. The demands and dream you had for a better life? The ambition that fueled your effort? These begin as earnest drives but left unchecked become hubris and entitlement. The same goes for the instinct to take charge; now you're addicted to control. Driven to prove the doubters wrong? Welcome to the seeds of paranoia.

Yes, there are legitimate stresses and anguish that come with the responsibilities of your new life. All the things you're managing, the frustrating mistakes of people who should know better, the endless creep of obligations—no one prepares us for that, which makes the feelings all the harder to deal with. The promised land was supposed to be nice, not aggravating. But you can't let the walls close in on you. You've got to get yourself—and your perceptions—under control.

When Arthur Lee was sent to France and England to serve as one of America's diplomats during the Revolutionary War, instead of relishing the opportunity to work with his fellow diplomat Silas Deane and elder statesman Benjamin Franklin, he raged and resented them and suspected them of disliking him. Finally, Franklin wrote him a letter (one that we've probably all deserved to get at one point or another): "If you do not cure yourself of this temper," Franklin advised, "it will end in insanity, of which it is the symptomatic forerunner." Probably because he was in such command of his own temper, Franklin decided that writing the letter was cathartic enough. He never sent it.

If you've ever listened to the Oval Office tapes of Richard Nixon, you can hear the same sickness, and you wish someone could have sent him such a letter. It's a harrowing insight into a man who has lost his grip not just on what he is legally allowed to do, on what his job was (to *serve* the people), but on reality itself. He vacillates wildly from supreme confidence to dread and fear. He talks over his subordinates and rejects information and feedback that challenges what he wants to believe. He lives in a bubble in which no one can say no—not even his conscience.

There's a letter from General Winfield Scott to Jefferson Davis, then the secretary of war for the United States. Davis belligerently pestered Scott repeatedly about some trivial matter. Scott ignored it until, finally, forced to address it, he wrote that he pitied Davis. "Compassion is always due," he said to him, "to an enraged imbecile, who lays about him in blows which hurt only himself."

Ego is its own worst enemy. It hurts the ones we love too. Our families and friends suffer for it. So do our customers, fans, and clients. A critic of Napoleon nailed it when remarking: "He despises the nation whose applause he seeks."

He couldn't help but see the French people as pieces to be manipulated, people he had to be better than, people who, unless they were totally, unconditionally supportive of him, were against him.

A smart man or woman must regularly remind themselves of the limits of their power and reach.

Entitlement assumes: This is mine. I've earned it. At the same time, entitlement nickels and dimes *other* people because it can't conceive of valuing another person's time as highly as its own. It delivers tirades and pronouncements that exhaust the people who work for and with us, who have no choice other than to go along. It overstates our abilities to ourselves, it renders generous judgment of our prospects, and it creates ridiculous expectations.

Control says, It all must be done *my* way—even little things, even inconsequential things. It can become paralyzing perfectionism, or a million pointless battles fought merely for the sake of exerting its say. It too exhausts people whose help we need, particularly quiet people who don't object until we've pushed them to their breaking point. We fight with the clerk at the airport, the customer service representative on the telephone, the agent who examines our claim. To what end? In reality, we don't control the weather, we don't control the market, we don't control other people, and our efforts and energies in spite of this are pure waste.

Paranoia thinks, I can't trust anyone. I'm in this totally by myself and for myself. It says, I'm surrounded by fools. It says, focusing on my work, my obligations, myself is not enough. I also have to be orchestrating various machinations behind the scenes—to get them before they get me; to get them back for the slights I perceive.

Everyone has had a boss, a partner, a parent like this. All that strife, anger, chaos, and conflict. How did it go for them? How did it end?

"He who indulges empty fears earns himself real fears," wrote Seneca, who as a political adviser witnessed destructive paranoia at the highest levels.

The sad feedback loop is that the relentless "looking out for number one" can encourage other people to undermine and fight us. They see that behavior for what it really is: a mask for weakness, insecurity, and instability. In its frenzy to protect itself, paranoia creates the persecution it seeks to avoid, making the owner a prisoner of its own delusions and chaos.

Is this the freedom you envisioned when you dreamed of your success? Likely not.

So stop.

MANAGING YOURSELF

It is not enough to have great qualities; we should also
have the management of them.

—LA ROCHEFOUCAULD

In 1953, Dwight D. Eisenhower returned from his inaugu-
ral parade and entered the White House for the first
time as president late in the evening. As he walked into
the Executive Mansion, his chief usher handed Eisenhower
two letters marked "Confidential and Secret" that had been
sent to him earlier in the day. Eisenhower's reaction was
swift: "Never bring me a sealed envelope," he said firmly.
"That's what I have a staff for."

How snobbish, right? Had the office really gone to his
head already?

Not at all. Eisenhower recognized the seemingly insignificant event for what it was: a symptom of a disorganized,
dysfunctional organization. Not everything needed to run
through him. Who was to say that the envelope was even
important? Why hadn't anyone screened it?

As president, his first priority in office was organizing the
executive branch into a smooth, functioning, and order-

driven unit, just like his military units had been—not because he didn't want to work himself, but because everyone had a job and he trusted and empowered them to do it. As his chief of staff later put it, "The president does the most important things. I do the *next* most important things."

The public image of Eisenhower is of the man playing golf. In reality, he was not someone who ever slacked off, but the leisure time he did have was available because he ran a tight ship. He knew that urgent and important were not synonyms. His job was to set the priorities, to think big picture, and then trust the people beneath him to do the jobs they were hired for.

Most of us are not *the* president, or even president of a *company*, but in moving up the ladder in life, the system and work habits that got us where we are won't necessarily keep us there. When we're aspiring or small time, we can be idiosyncratic, we can compensate for disorganization with hard work and a little luck. That's not going to cut it in the majors. In fact, it'll sink you if you can't grow up and *organize*.

We can contrast Eisenhower's system in the White House with the infamous car company created by John DeLorean, when he walked away from GM to produce his brand of futuristic cars. A few decades removed from the company's spectacular implosion, we can be forgiven for thinking the man was just ahead of his time. In fact, his rise and fall is as timeless a story as there is: Power-hungry narcissist undermines his own vision, and loses millions of dollars of other people's money in the process.

DeLorean was convinced that the culture of order and discipline at GM had held brilliant creatives like himself down.

When he set out to found his company, he deliberately did everything differently, flouting conventional wisdom and business practices. The result was not the freewheeling, creative sanctuary that DeLorean naively envisioned. It was, instead, an overbearingly political, dysfunctional, and even corrupt organization that collapsed under its own weight, eventually resorting to criminality and fraud, and losses of some $250 million.

The DeLorean failed both as a car and as a company because it was mismanaged from top to bottom—with an emphasis on the mismanagement at the top, by the top. That is: DeLorean himself was the problem. Compared to Eisenhower, he worked constantly, with very different results.

As one executive put it, DeLorean "had the ability to recognize a good opportunity but he didn't know how to make it happen." Another executive described his management style as "chasing colored balloons"—he was constantly distracted and abandoning one project for another. He was a genius. Sadly, that's rarely enough.

Though probably not on purpose, DeLorean created a culture in which ego ran free. Convinced that continued success was simply his by right, he seemed to bristle at concepts like discipline, organization, or strategic planning. Employees were not given enough direction, and then at other times, overwhelmed with trivial instructions. DeLorean couldn't delegate—except to lackeys whose blind loyalty was prized over competence or skill. On top of all this, he was often late or preoccupied.

Executives were allowed to work on extracurricular activities on the company dime, encouraged specifically to chase side projects that benefited their boss at the expense of the company. As CEO, DeLorean often bent the truth to investors, fellow officers, and suppliers, and this habit was contagious throughout the company.

Like many people driven by a demon, DeLorean's decisions were motivated by everything *but* what would have been efficient, manageable, or responsible. Instead of improving or fixing GM's system, it's as if he threw out order altogether. What ensued was chaos in which no one followed the rules, no one was accountable, and very little got done. The only reason it didn't collapse immediately was that DeLorean was a master of public relations—a skill that held the whole story together until the first faulty cars came off the assembly line.

Not surprisingly, the cars were *terrible*. They didn't work. Cost per unit was massively over budget. They hadn't secured enough dealers. They couldn't deliver cars to the ones they had. The launch was a disaster. DeLorean Motor Company never recovered.

It turns out that becoming a great leader is difficult. *Who knew?!*

DeLorean couldn't manage himself, and so he had trouble managing others. And so he managed to fail, both himself and the dream.

Management? That's the reward for all your creativity and new ideas? Becoming the Man? Yes—in the end, we all face becoming the adult supervision we originally rebelled against. Yet often we react petulantly and prefer to think: *Now that I'm in charge, things are going to be different!*

Think about Eisenhower. He was the damn president—the most powerful man in the world. He could have kicked back and done things how he liked. If he was disorganized, people would have just had to deal with it (there have been plenty of those presidents before). Yet he wasn't. He understood that order and responsibility were what the country needed. And that this far outweighed his own concerns.

What was so sad about DeLorean is that, like a lot of talented people, his ideas were on point. His car was an exciting innovation. His model could have worked. He had all the assets and the talent. It was his ego and the disorganization that resulted from it that prevented the ingredients from coming together—just as it they do for so many of us.

As you become successful in your own field, your responsibilities may begin to change. Days become less and less about *doing* and more and more about making decisions. Such is the nature of leadership. This transition requires reevaluating and updating your identity. It requires a certain humility to put aside some of the more enjoyable or satisfying parts of your previous job. It means accepting that others might be more qualified or specialized in areas in which you considered yourself competent—or at least their time is better spent on them than yours.

Yes, it would be more fun to be constantly involved in every tiny matter, and might make us feel important to be the person called to put out fires. The little things are endlessly engaging and often flattering, while the big picture can be hard to discern. It's not always fun, but it is the job. If you don't think big picture—because you're too busy playing "boss man"—who will?

Of course, there is no "right" system. Sometimes systems are better decentralized. Sometimes they are better in a strict hierarchy. Every project and goal deserves an approach fitted perfectly to what needs to be done. Maybe a creative, relaxed environment makes the most sense for what you're doing. Maybe you can run your business remotely, or maybe it's better for everyone to see each other face-to-face.

What matters is that you learn how to manage yourself and others, before your industry eats you alive. Micromanagers are egotists who can't manage others and they quickly get overloaded. So do the charismatic visionaries who lose interest when it's time to execute. Worse yet are those who surround themselves with yes-men or sycophants who clean up their messes and create a bubble in which they can't even see how disconnected from reality they are.

Responsibility requires a readjustment and then *increased* clarity and purpose. First, setting the top-level goals and priorities of the organization and your life. Then enforcing and observing them. To produce results and only results.

A fish stinks from the head, is the saying. Well, you're the head now.

BEWARE THE DISEASE OF ME

> If I am not for myself who will be for me? If I am only for myself, who am I?
>
> —HILLEL

There were great Allied generals of World War II—Patton, Bradley, Montgomery, Eisenhower, MacArthur, Zhukov—and then there was George Catlett Marshall Jr. Although all of them served their countries and fought and led bravely, one stands apart.

Today, we see World War II as a clear fight in which good aligned selflessly against evil. The problem is that victory and the passage of time have obscured the all-too-humanness of the people who were on the right side of that fight. That is: we forget the politics, the backstabbing, the spotlight coveting, the posturing, the greed, and the ass-covering among the Allies. While the other generals protected their turf, fought with each other, and eagerly aspired to their place in history, that behavior was virtually absent in one man: General George Marshall.

More impressively, Marshall quietly outpaced all of them

with the magnitude of his accomplishments. What was his secret?

Pat Riley, the famous coach and manager who led the Los Angeles Lakers and Miami Heat to multiple championships, says that great teams tend to follow a trajectory. When they start—before they have won—a team is innocent. If the conditions are right, they come together, they watch out for each other and work together toward their collective goal. This stage, he calls the "Innocent Climb."

After a team starts to win and media attention begins, the simple bonds that joined the individuals together begin to fray. Players calculate their own importance. Chests swell. Frustrations emerge. Egos appear. The Innocent Climb, Pat Riley says, is almost always followed by the "Disease of Me." It can "strike any winning team in any year and at any moment," and does with alarming regularity.

It's Shaq and Kobe, unable to play together. It's Jordan punching Steve Kerr, Jud Buechler, *and* Will Perdue—his own team members. He punched people on his own team! It's Enron employees plunging California into darkness for personal profit. It's leaks to the media from a disgruntled executive hoping to scuttle a project he dislikes. It's negging and every other intimidation tactic.

For us, it's beginning to think that we're better, that we're special, that our problems and experiences are so incredibly different from everyone else's that no one could possibly understand. It's an attitude that has sunk far better people, teams, and causes than ours.

With General Marshall, who began his term as chief of staff of the U.S. Army on the day Germany invaded Poland in 1939 and served through the entire war, we see one of history's few exceptions to this trend. Marshall somehow never caught the Disease of Me, and in many ways, often shamed it out of the people who did.

It begins with his balanced relationship to rank, an obsession for most people in his line of work.

He was not a man who abstained from *every* public show of rank or status. He insisted that the president call him General Marshall, not George, for example. (He earned it, right?) But while other generals regularly lobbied for promotions—General MacArthur advanced over other officers in the prewar years largely due to the aggressive efforts of *his mother*—Marshall actively discouraged it. When others began to push for Marshall to be chief of staff, he asked them to stop, because "[it] makes me conspicuous in the army. Too conspicuous in fact." Later, he discouraged an effort by the House to pass a bill awarding him the rank of field marshal—not only because he thought the name Field Marshal *Marshall* would sound ridiculous, but because he didn't want to outrank or hurt his mentor, General Pershing, who was near death and a constant source of advice and guidance.

Can you imagine? In all these cases, his sense of honor meant turning down honors, and often letting them go to other people. Like any normal human being, he wanted them, only the right way. More important, he knew that, however nice they would have been to have, he could do without them while perhaps others could not. Ego needs honors in order to be validated. Confidence, on the other hand, is able to wait and focus on the task at hand regardless of external recognition.

Early on in our careers, we may be able to make these

sacrifices more easily. We can drop out of a prestigious college to start our own company. Or we can tolerate being looked over once in a while. Once we've "made it," the tendency is to switch to the mind-set of "getting what's mine." Now, all of a sudden awards and recognition matter—even though they weren't what got us here. We *need* that money, that title, that media attention—not for the team or the cause, but for ourselves. Because we've *earned* it.

Let's make one thing clear: we never earn the right to be greedy or to pursue our interests at the expense of everyone else. To think otherwise is not only egotistical, it's counterproductive.

Marshall was tested on this to the extreme. A job he'd trained his whole life for was up for grabs: command of the troops on D-Day, essentially the largest coordinated invasion the world had ever seen. Roosevelt let it be known that it was Marshall's if he wanted it. A general's place in history is assured by his feats in battle, so even though Marshall was needed in Washington, Roosevelt wanted to give him the opportunity to take command. Marshall would have none of it. "The decision is yours, Mr. President; my wishes have nothing to do with the matter." The role and the glory went to Eisenhower.

It came to be that Eisenhower was, in fact, the best man for that job. He performed superbly and helped win the war. Would anything else have been worth the trade-off?

Yet this is what we regularly refuse to do; our ego precludes serving any larger mission we're a part of.

What are we going to do? Let someone get one over on us?

The writer Cheryl Strayed once told a young reader, "You're becoming who you are going to be and so you might as well not be an asshole." This is one of the most dangerous ironies of success—it can make us someone we never wanted to be in the first place. The Disease of Me can corrupt the most innocent climb.

There was a general who treated Marshall poorly—essentially banishing him to some obscure postings in the middle of his career. Later, Marshall surpassed him and had his chance for revenge. Except—he didn't take it. Because whatever the man's flaws, Marshall saw that he was still of use and that the country would be worse off without him. What were the thanks for this quiet suppression of ego? Just another job well done—and not much more.

The word for that is one we don't use much anymore: magnanimous. It was good strategy too, of course, but mostly Marshall was gracious, forgiving, and magnanimous because it was right. According to observers as high up as President Truman, what separated Marshall from nearly everyone else in the military and politics is that "never did General Marshall think about himself."

There is another story of Marshall sitting for one of the many official portraits that was required of him. After appearing many times and patiently honoring the requests, Marshall was finally informed by the painter that he was finished and free to go. Marshall stood up and began to leave. "Don't you want to see the painting?" the artist asked. "No, thank you," Marshall said respectfully and left.

Is that to say that managing your image isn't important? Of course not. Early in your career, you'll notice that you jump on every opportunity to do so. As you become more accomplished, you'll realize that so much of it is a distraction from your work—time spent with reporters, with awards, and with marketing are time away from what you really care about.

Who has time to look at a picture of himself? What's the point?

As his wife later observed, the people who saw George Marshall as simply modest or quiet missed what was special about the man. He had the same traits that everyone has—ego, self-interest, pride, dignity, ambition—but they were "tempered by a sense of humility and selflessness."

It doesn't make you a bad person to want to be remembered. To want to make it to the top. To provide for yourself and your family. After all, that's all part of the allure.

There is a balance. Soccer coach Tony Adams expresses it well. Play for the name on the front of the jersey, he says, and they'll remember the name on the back.

When it comes to Marshall, the old idea that selflessness and integrity could be weaknesses or hold someone back are laughably disproven. Sure, some people might have trouble telling you much about him—but each and every one of them lives in a world he was largely responsible for shaping.

The credit? Who cares.

MEDITATE ON THE IMMENSITY

A monk is a man who is separated from all and who is in harmony with all.

—EVAGRIUS PONTICUS

In 1879, the preservationist and explorer John Muir took his first trip to Alaska. As he explored the fjords and rocky landscapes of Alaska's now famous Glacier Bay, a powerful feeling struck him all at once. He'd always been in love with nature, and here in the unique summer climate of the far north, in this single moment, it was as if the entire world was in sync. As if he could see the entire ecosystem and circle of life before him. His pulse began to pick up, and he and the group were "warmed and quickened into sympathy with everything, taken back into the heart of nature" from which we all came. Thankfully, Muir noticed and recorded in his journal the beautiful cohesion of the world around him, which few have ever matched since.

We feel the life and motion about us, and the universal beauty: the tides marching back and forth with weariless industry, laving the beautiful shores, and swaying the purple dulse of the broad meadows of the sea where the fishes are fed, the wild streams in rows white with waterfalls, ever in bloom and ever in song, spreading their branches over a thousand mountains; the vast forests feeding on the drenching sunbeams, every cell in a whirl of enjoyment; misty flocks of insects stirring all the air, the wild sheep and goats on the grassy ridges above the woods, bears in the berry-tangles, mink and beaver and otter far back on many a river and lake; Indians and adventurers pursuing their lonely ways; birds tending to their young—everywhere, everywhere, beauty and life, and glad, rejoicing action.

In this moment, he was experiencing what the Stoics would call *sympatheia*—a connectedness with the cosmos. The French philosopher Pierre Hadot has referred to it as the "oceanic feeling." A sense of belonging to something larger, of realizing that "human things are an infinitesimal point in the immensity." It is in these moments that we're not only free but drawn toward important questions: *Who am I? What am I doing? What is my role in this world?*

Nothing draws us away from those questions like material success—when we are always busy, stressed, put upon, distracted, reported to, relied on, apart from. When we're wealthy and told that we're important or powerful. Ego tells us that meaning comes from activity, that being the center of attention is the only way to matter.

When we lack a connection to anything larger or bigger than us, it's like a piece of our soul is gone. Like we've detached ourselves from the traditions we hail from, whatever that happens to be (a craft, a sport, a brotherhood or sister-hood, a family). Ego blocks us from the beauty and history in the world. It stands in the way.

No wonder we find success empty. No wonder we're exhausted. No wonder it feels like we're on a treadmill. No wonder we lose touch with the energy that once fueled us.

Here's an exercise: walk onto ancient battlefield or a place of historical significance. Look at the statues and you can't help but see how similar the people look, how little has changed since then—since before, and how it will be forever after. Here a great man once stood. Here another brave woman died. Here a cruel rich man lived, in this palatial home . . . It's the sense that others have been here before you, generations of them, in fact.

In those moments, we have a sense of the immensity of the world. Ego is impossible, because we realize, if only fleet-ingly, what Emerson meant when he said that "Every man is a quotation from all his ancestors." They are part of us, we are part of a tradition. Embrace the power of this position and learn from it. It is an exhilarating feeling to grasp this, like the one that Muir felt in Alaska. Yes, we are small. We are also a piece of this great universe and a process.

The astrophysicist Neil deGrasse Tyson has described this duality well—it's possible to bask in both your relevance and irrelevance to the cosmos. As he says, "When I look up in the universe, I know I'm small, but I'm also big. I'm big because I'm connected to the universe and the universe is connected to me." We just can't forget which is bigger and which has been here longer.

Why do you think that great leaders and thinkers throughout history have "gone out into the wilderness" and come back with inspiration, with a plan, with an experience that puts them on a course that changes the world? It's because in doing so they found perspective, they understood the larger picture in a way that wasn't possible in the bustle of everyday life. Silencing the noise around them, they could finally hear the quiet voice they needed to listen to.

Creativity is a matter of receptiveness and recognition. This cannot happen if you're convinced the world revolves around you.

By removing the ego—even temporarily—we can access what's left standing in relief. By widening our perspective, more comes into view.

It's sad how disconnected from the past and the future most of us really are. We forget that woolly mammoths walked the earth while the pyramids were being built. We don't realize that Cleopatra lived closer to our time than she did to the construction of those famous pyramids that marked her kingdom. When British workers excavated the land in Trafalgar Square to build Nelson's Column and its famous stone lions, in the ground they found the bones of *actual* lions, who'd roamed that exact spot just a few thousand years before. Someone recently calculated that it takes but a chain of six individuals who shook hands with one another across the centuries to connect Barack Obama to George Washington. There's a video you can watch on YouTube of a man on a CBS game show, "I've Got a Secret," in 1956, in an episode that also happened to feature a famous actress named Lucille Ball. His secret? He was in Ford's Theatre when Lincoln was assassinated. England's government only recently paid off debts it incurred as far back as 1720 from events like the South Sea Bubble, the Napoleonic wars, the empire's abolition of slavery, and the Irish potato famine—meaning that in the twenty-first century there was still a direct and daily connection to the eighteenth and nineteenth centuries.

As our power or talents grow, we like to think that makes us special—that we live in blessed, unprecedented times. This is compounded by the fact that so many of the photos we see from even fifty years ago are still in black and white, and we seem to assume that the *world* was in black and white. Obviously, it wasn't—their sky was the same color as ours (in some places brighter than ours), they bled the same way we did, and their cheeks got flushed just like ours do. We are just like them, and always will be.

"It's hard to be humble when you're as great as I am," Muhammad Ali once said. Yeah, okay. That's why great people have to work even harder to fight against this headwind. It's hard to be self-absorbed and convinced of your own greatness inside the solitude and quiet of a sensory deprivation tank. It's hard to be anything *but* humble walking alone along a beach late at night with an endless black ocean crashing loudly against the ground next to you.

We have to actively seek out this cosmic sympathy. There's the famous Blake poem that opens with "To see a World in a Grain of Sand / And a Heaven in a Wild Flower / Hold Infinity in the palm of your hand / And Eternity in an hour." That's what we're after here. That's the transcendental experience that makes our petty ego impossible.

Feel unprotected against the elements or forces or surroundings. Remind yourself how pointless it is to rage and fight and try to one-up those around you. Go and put yourself in touch with the infinite, and end your conscious separation from the world. Reconcile yourself a bit better with the realities of life. Realize how much came before you, and how only wisps of it remain.

Let the feeling carry you as long as you can. Then when you start to feel better or bigger than, go and do it again.

MAINTAIN YOUR SOBRIETY

The height of cultivation runs to simplicity.

—BRUCE LEE

Angela Merkel is the antithesis of nearly every assumption we make about a head of state—especially a German one. She is plain. She is modest. She cares little for presentation or flash. She gives no fiery speeches. She has no interest in expansion or domination. Mostly, she is quiet and reserved.

Chancellor Angela Merkel is *sober*, when far too many leaders are intoxicated—with ego, with power, with position. This sobriety is precisely what has made her a wildly popular three-term leader and, paradoxically, a powerful, sweeping force for freedom and peace in modern Europe.

There is a story about Merkel as a young girl, at a swimming lesson. She walked out on the diving board and stood there, thinking about whether she should jump. Minutes ticked by. More minutes. Finally, just as the bell marking the end of the lesson began to ring, she jumped. Was she afraid or just cautious? Many years later, she would remind Europe's leaders during a major crisis that "Fear is a bad advisor." As a kid on that diving board, she wanted to use every allotted second to make the *right* decision, not driven by recklessness or fear.

In most cases, we think that people become successful through sheer energy and enthusiasm. We almost excuse ego because we think it's part and parcel of the personality required to "make it big." Maybe a bit of that overpowering-ness is what got you where you are. But let's ask: Is it really sustainable for the next several decades? Can you really outwork and outrun everyone *forever*?

The answer is no. The ego tells us we're invincible, that we have unlimited force that will never dissipate. But that can't be what greatness requires—energy without end?

Merkel is the embodiment of Aesop's fable about the tortoise. She is slow and steady. The historic night the Berlin Wall fell, she was thirty-five. She had one beer, went to bed, and showed up early for work the next day. A few years later, she had worked to become a respected but obscure physicist. Only then did she enter politics. In her fifties, she became chancellor. It was a diligent, plodding path.

Yet the rest of us want to get to the top as fast as humanly possible. We have no patience for waiting. We're high on getting high up the ranks. Once we've made it, we tend to think that ego and energy is the only way to stay there. It's not.

When Russian president Vladimir Putin once attempted to intimidate Merkel by letting his large hunting dog barge into a meeting (she is reportedly not a dog lover), she didn't flinch and later joked about it. As a result, he was the one who looked foolish and insecure. During her rise and especially during her time in power, she has consistently maintained her equilibrium and clearheadedness, regardless of the immediate stressors or stimuli.

In a similar position, we might have sprung into "bold" action; we might have gotten angry or drawn a line in the sand. We have to stand up for ourselves, right? But do we? So often, this is just ego, escalating tension more than dealing with it. Merkel is firm, clear, and patient. She's willing to compromise on everything except the principle at stake—which far too many people lose sight of.

That is sobriety. That is command of oneself.

She did not become the most powerful woman in the Western world by accident. More importantly, she's maintained her perch for three terms with the same formula.

The great philosopher king Marcus Aurelius knew this very well. Called to politics almost against his will, he served the Roman people in continually higher offices from his teens until his death. There was always pressing business— appeals to hear, wars to fight, laws to pass, favors to grant. He strove to escape what he called "imperialization"—the stain of absolute power that had wrecked previous emperors. To do that, he wrote *to himself*, he must "fight to be the person philosophy tried to make you."

This is why the Zen philosopher Zuigan is supposed to have called out to himself everyday:

"MASTER—"
"YES, SIR?"

Then he would add:

"BECOME SOBER."
"YES, SIR."

He would conclude by saying:

"DO NOT BE DECEIVED BY OTHERS."
"YES SIR, YES SIR."

Today, we might add to that:

"DON'T BE DECEIVED BY RECOGNITION YOU HAVE GOTTEN OR THE AMOUNT OF MONEY IN YOUR BANK ACCOUNT."

We have to fight to stay sober, despite the many different forces swirling around our ego.

The historian Shelby Foote observed that "power doesn't so much corrupt; that's too simple. It fragments, closes options, mesmerizes." That's what ego does. It clouds the mind precisely when it needs to be clear. Sobriety is a counterbalance, a hangover cure—or better, a prevention method.

Other politicians are bold and charismatic. But as Merkel supposedly said, "You can't solve . . . tasks with charisma." She is rational. She analyzes. She makes it about the situation, not about herself, as people in power often do. Her background in science is helpful here, surely. Politicians are often vain, obsessing about their image. Merkel is too objective for that. She cares about results and little else. A German writer observed in a tribute on her fiftieth birthday that *unpretentiousness* is Merkel's main weapon.

David Halberstam, writing about the Patriots' coach Bill

Belichick, observed that the man was "not only in the steak business, he had contempt for sizzle." You could say the same about Merkel. Leaders like Belichick and Merkel know that steak is what wins games and moves nations forward. Sizzle, on the other hand, makes it harder to make the *right* decisions—how to interact with others, who to promote, which plays to run, what feedback to listen to, where to come down on an issue.

Churchill's Europe required one type of leader. Today's interconnected world requires its own. Because there is so much information to be sorted through, so much competition, so much change, without a clear head . . . all is lost.

We're not talking about abstinence from drugs or alcohol obviously, but there certainly is an element of restraint to egoless sobriety—an elimination of the unnecessary and the destructive. No more obsessing about your image; treating people beneath you or above you with contempt; needing first-class trappings and the star treatment; raging, fighting, preening, performing, lording over, condescending, and marveling at your own awesomeness or self-anointed importance.

Sobriety is the counterweight that must balance out success. Especially if things keep getting better and better.

As James Basford remarked, "It requires a strong constitution to withstand repeated attacks of prosperity." Well, that's where we are now.

There's an old line about how if you want to live happy, live hidden. It's true. The problem is, that means the rest of us are deprived of really good examples. We're lucky to see someone like Merkel in the public eye, because she is the representative of a very large, silent majority.

As hard as it might be to believe from what we see in the

media, there actually are some successful people with modest apartments. Like Merkel, they have normal private lives with their spouses (her husband skipped her first inauguration). They lack artifice, they wear normal clothes. Most successful people are people you've never heard of. They want it that way.

It keeps them sober. It helps them do their jobs.

FOR WHAT OFTEN COMES NEXT,
EGO IS THE ENEMY . . .

The evidence is in, and you are the verdict.

—ANNE LAMOTT

Here you are at the pinnacle. What have you found? Just how tough and tricky it is to manage. You thought it would get easier when you arrived; instead, it's even harder—a different animal entirely. What you found is that you must manage yourself in order to maintain your success.

The philosopher Aristotle was not unfamiliar with the worlds of ego and power and empire. His most famous pupil was Alexander the Great, and partially through Aristotle's teachings, the young man conquered the entire known world. Alexander was brave and brilliant and often generous and wise. Still, it's clear that he ignored Aristotle's most important lesson—and that's partially why he died at age thirty-two, far from home, likely killed by his own men, who had finally said, "Enough."

It's not that he was wrong to have great ambitions. Alexander just never grasped Aristotle's "golden mean"—that is, the middle ground. Repeatedly, Aristotle speaks of virtue and excellence as points along a spectrum. Courage, for instance, lies between cowardice on one end and recklessness on the other. Generosity, which we all admire, must stop short of either profligacy and parsimony in order to be of any use. Where the line—this golden mean—is can be difficult to tell, but without finding it, we risk dangerous extremes. This is why it is so hard to be excellent, Aristotle wrote. "In each case, it is hard work to find the intermediate; for instance, not everyone, but only one who knows, finds the midpoint in a circle."

We can use the golden mean to navigate our ego and our desire to achieve.

Endless ambition is easy; anyone can put their foot down hard on the gas. Complacency is easy too; it's just a matter of taking that foot *off* the gas. We must avoid what the business strategist Jim Collins terms the "undisciplined pursuit of more," as well as the complacency that comes with plaudits. To borrow from Aristotle again, what's difficult is to apply the right amount of pressure, at the right time, in the right way, for the right period of time, in the right car, going in the right direction.

If we don't do this, the consequences can be dire.

There is a line from Napoleon, who, like Alexander, died miserably. He said, "Men of great ambition have sought happiness . . . and have found fame." What he means is that behind every goal is the drive to be happy and fulfilled—but when egotism takes hold, we lose track of our goal and end up somewhere we never intended. Emerson, in his famous essay on Napoleon, takes pains to point out that just a few years after his death, Europe was essentially exactly as it was before Napoleon began his precipitous rise. All that death, that effort, that greed, and those honors—for what? For basically nothing. Napoleon, he wrote, quickly faded away, just like the smoke from his artillery.

Howard Hughes—despite his current reputation as some kind of bold maverick—was not a happy man, no matter how awesome his life may seem from history or movies. When he was near death, one of his aides sought to reassure a suffering Hughes. "What an incredible life you have led," the aide said. Hughes shook his head and replied with the sad, emphatic honesty of someone whose time has clearly come, "If you had ever swapped places in life with me, I would be willing to bet that you would have demanded to swap back before the passage of the first week."

We do not have to follow in those footsteps. We know what decisions we must make to avoid that ignominious, even pathetic end: protecting our sobriety, eschewing greed and paranoia, staying humble, retaining our sense of purpose, connecting to the larger world around us.

Because even if we manage ourselves well, prosperity holds no guarantees. The world conspires against us in many ways, and the laws of nature say that everything regresses toward the mean. In sports, the schedule gets harder after a winning season, the bad teams get better draft picks, and the salary cap makes it tough to keep a team together. In life, taxes go up the more you make, and the more obligations society foists on you. The media is harder on those it has covered before. Rumors and gossip are the cost of renown: He's a drunk. She's gay. He's a hypocrite. She's a bitch. The crowd roots for the underdog, and roots *against* the winners.

These are just facts of life. Who can afford to add denial to all that?

Instead of letting power make us delusional and instead of taking what we have for granted, we'd be better to spend our time preparing for the shifts of fate that inevitably occur in life. That is, adversity, difficulty, failure.

Who knows—maybe a downturn is exactly what's coming next. Worse, maybe you caused it. Just because you did something once, doesn't mean you'll be able to do it successfully forever.

Reversals and regressions are as much a part of the cycle of life as anything else.

But we can manage that too.

PART III

FAILURE

Here we are experiencing the trials endemic to any journey.
Perhaps we've failed, perhaps our goal turned out to be harder
to achieve than anticipated. No one is permanently successful,
and not everyone finds success on the first attempt. We all deal
with setbacks along the way. Ego not only leaves us unprepared
for these circumstances, it often contributed to their occurrence in the first place. The way through, the way to rise again,
requires a reorientation and increased self-awareness. We
don't need pity—our own or anyone else's—we need purpose,
poise, and patience.

TO WHATEVER FAILURE AND
CHALLENGES YOU WILL FACE,
EGO IS THE ENEMY . . .

It is because mankind are disposed to sympathize more entirely with our joy than with our sorrow, that we make parade of our riches, and conceal our poverty. Nothing is so mortifying as to be obliged to expose our distress to the view of the public, and to feel, that though our situation is open to the eyes of all mankind, no mortal conceives for us the half of what we suffer.

—ADAM SMITH

For the first half of her life, Katharine Graham saw pretty much everything go right.

Her father, Eugene Meyer, was a financial genius who made a fortune in the stock market. Her mother was a beautiful as well as brilliant socialite. As a child, Katharine had the best of everything: the best schools, the best teachers, big houses, and servants to wait on her.

In 1933, her father bought the *Washington Post*, then a struggling but important newspaper, which he began to turn around. The only child to express any serious interest in it, Katharine inherited the paper when she was older and handed over the management to her equally impressive husband, Philip Graham.

She was not another Howard Hughes, who squandered

her family's fortune. She was not another rich kid who took the easy road in life because she could. But it was a cushy life, no question about it. She had been, in her words, content to be the tail to her husband's (and parent's) kite.

Then life took a turn. Phil Graham's behavior became increasingly erratic. He drank heavily. He made reckless business decisions and bought things they couldn't afford. He began having affairs. He publicly humiliated his wife in front of nearly everyone they knew. Rich people problems, right? It turns out that he had suffered a severe mental breakdown, and as Katharine attempted to nurse him back to health, he killed himself with a hunting rifle while she napped in the next room.

In 1963, at forty-six years old, Katharine Graham, a mother of three with no work experience, found herself in charge of the Washington Post Company, a vast corporation with thousands of employees. She was unprepared, timid, and naive.

Though tragic, these events were not exactly a cataclysmic failure. Graham was still rich, still white, still privileged. Still, it was not what she thought life had planned for her. That's the point. Failure and adversity are relative and unique to each of us. Almost without exception, this is what life does: it takes our plans and dashes them to pieces. Sometimes once, sometimes lots of times.

As the financial philosopher and economist George Goodman once observed, it is as if "we are at a wonderful ball where the champagne sparkles in every glass and soft laughter falls upon the summer air. We know at some moment the black horsemen will come shattering through the terrace doors wreaking vengeance and scattering the survivors. Those who leave early are saved, but the ball is so splendid no one wants to leave while there is still time. So everybody keeps asking—what time is it? But none of the clocks have hands."

He was speaking of economic crises, although he may as well have been talking about where all of us find ourselves, not just once in our lifetimes, but often. Things are going well. Perhaps we're aspiring to some big goal. Perhaps we're finally enjoying the fruits of our labors. At any point, fate can intervene.

If success is ego intoxication, then failure can be a devastating ego blow—turning slips into falls and little troubles into great unravelings. If ego is often just a nasty side effect of great success, it can be fatal during failure.

We have many names for these problems: Sabotage. Unfairness. Adversity. Trials. Tragedy. No matter the label, it's a trial. We don't like it, and some of us are sunk by it. Others seem to be built to make it through. In either case, it's a trial each person must endure.

This fate is as much written for us as it was written five thousand years ago for the young king in *Gilgamesh*:

> *He will face a battle he knows not,*
> *he will ride a road he knows not.*

That's what came to Katharine Graham. It turned out that taking over the paper was the first in a series of trying and wrenching events that lasted for nearly two decades.

Thomas Paine, remarking about George Washington, once wrote that there is a "natural firmness in some minds which cannot be unlocked by trifles, but which, when unlocked, discovers a cabinet of fortitude." Graham seems to have possessed a similar cabinet.

As she settled into her leadership position, Graham found that the paper's conservative board was a constant obstacle. They were patronizing and risk averse and had held the company back. To succeed, she would have to develop her own compass and not defer to others the way she always had. It eventually became clear that she needed a new executive editor. Against the board's advice, she replaced the well-liked good old boy with an unknown young upstart. Simple enough.

The next turn of the screw wasn't. Just as the company was filing to go public, the *Post* received a collection of stolen government documents that editors asked Graham if they could run, despite a court order preventing their publication. She consulted the company's lawyers. She consulted the board. All advised against it—fearing it could sink the IPO or tie the company up in lawsuits for years. Torn, she decided to proceed and publish them—a decision with essentially no precedent. Shortly thereafter, the paper's investigation of a burglary at the Democratic National Committee's headquarters—relying on an anonymous source—threatened to put the company permanently at odds with the White House and Washington's powerful elite (as well as jeopardizing the government licenses they needed for the TV stations the *Post* owned). At one point, Nixon loyalist and the *attorney general of the United States* John Mitchell threatened that Graham had so overreached that her "tit" was going to be "caught in a big fat wringer." Another aide bragged that the White House was now thinking about how to screw the paper over. Put yourself in her shoes: the most powerful office in the world explicitly strategizing, "How can we hurt the *Post* the most?"

On top of that, the *Post*'s stock price was less than stellar. The market was poor. In 1974, an investor began aggressively buying up shares in the company. The board was terrified. It could mean a hostile takeover. Graham was dispatched to deal with him. The following year, the paper's printers' union began a vicious, protracted strike. At one point, union members wore shirts that said, "Phil Shot the Wrong Graham." Despite—or perhaps because of—these tactics, she decided to fight the strike. They fought back. At four o'clock one morning came a a frantic call: the union had sabotaged company machinery, beaten up an innocent staffer, and then set one of the printing presses on fire. Typically, during printing strikes competitors will help fellow papers out with their printing but Graham's competitors refused, costing the *Post* $300,000 a day in advertising revenue.

Then, a suite of major investors began to sell their stock positions in the Washington Post Company, ostensibly having lost their faith in its prospects. Graham, pushed by the activist investor she'd met with earlier, decided her best option was to spend an enormous amount of the company's money to buy back its own shares on the public markets—a dangerous move that almost no one was doing at the time.

That's a list of problems exhausting to read about let alone live through. Yet because of Graham's perseverance, it shook out better than anyone could have possibly predicted.

The leaked documents Katharine Graham published

became known as the Pentagon Papers and were one of the most important stories in the history of journalism. The paper's Watergate reporting, which so incensed the Nixon White House, changed American history and took down an entire administration. It also won the paper a Pulitzer Prize. The investor others had feared turned out to be a young Warren Buffett, who became her business mentor and an enormous advocate and steward of the company. (His small investments in her family's company would one day be worth hundreds of millions.) She prevailed in negotiations with the union and the strike eventually ended. Her main competitor in Washington, the one that had refused to come to her aid, the *Star*, suddenly folded and was acquired by the *Post*. Her stock buybacks—made contrary not only to business wisdom, but the judgment of the market—made the company *billions* of dollars.

It turns out that the long hard slog she endured, the mistakes she made, the repeated failures, crises, and attacks were all leading somewhere. If you'd invested $1 in the *Post*'s IPO in 1971, it would be worth $89 by the time Graham stepped down in 1993—compared to $14 for her industry and $5 for the S&P 500. It makes her not just one of the most successful female CEOs of her generation and the first to run a Fortune 500 company, but one of the best CEOs ever, period.

For someone born with a silver spoon in her mouth, the first decade and a half was what you'd call a baptism of fire. Graham faced difficulty after difficulty, difficulties that she wasn't really equipped to handle, or so it seemed. There were times when it probably felt like she should have just sold the damn thing and enjoyed her massive wealth.

Graham didn't cause her husband's suicide, but it was left to her to carry on without him. She didn't ask for Watergate and the Pentagon Papers, but it fell on her to navigate their incendiary nature. While others went on buying and merger sprees in the eighties, she didn't. She doubled down on herself and her own company, despite the fact that it was treated as a weakling by Wall Street. She could have taken the easy way a hundred times, but did not.

At any given moment, there is the chance of failure or setbacks. Bill Walsh says, "Almost always, your road to victory goes through a place called 'failure.'" In order to taste success again, we've got to understand what led to this moment (or these years) of difficulty, what went wrong and why. We must deal with the situation in order to move past it. We'll need to accept it *and* to push through it.

Graham was alone in most of this. She was blindly feeling her way through the dark, trying to figure out a tough situation she never expected to be in. She's an example of how you can do most everything right and still find yourself in deep shit.

We think that failure only comes to egomaniacs who were begging for it. Nixon deserved to fail; did Graham? The reality is that while yes, often people set themselves up to crash, good people fail (or other people fail them) all the time too. People who have already been through a lot find themselves stuck with more. Life isn't fair.

Ego loves this notion, the idea that something is "fair" or not. Psychologists call it narcissistic injury when we take personally totally indifferent and objective events. We do that when our sense of self is fragile and dependent on life going our way all the time. Whether what you're going through is your fault or your problem doesn't matter, because it's yours to deal with right now. Graham's ego didn't cause her to fail, but if she'd had one, it certainly would have prevented her from succeeding ever again. You could say that failure always arrives uninvited, but through our ego, far too many of us allow it to stick around.

What did Graham need through all this? Not swagger. Not bluster. She needed to be strong. She needed confidence and a willingness to endure. A sense of right and wrong. *Purpose.* It wasn't about *her.* It was about preserving her family's legacy. Protecting the paper. Doing her job.

What about you? Will your ego betray you when things get difficult? Or can you proceed without it?

When we face difficulty, particularly public difficulty (doubters, scandals, losses), our friend the ego will show its true colors.

Absorbing the negative feedback, ego says: I knew you couldn't do it. *Why did you ever try?* It claims: This isn't worth it. This isn't fair. This is somebody else's problem. *Why don't you come up with a good excuse and wash your hands of this?* It tells us we shouldn't have to put up with this. It tells us that we're not the problem.

That is, it adds self-injury to every injury you experience.

To paraphrase Epicurus, the narcissistically inclined live in an "unwalled city." A fragile sense of self is constantly under threat. Illusions and accomplishments are not defenses, not when you've got the special sensitive antennae trained to receive (and create) the signals that challenge your precarious balancing act.

It is a miserable way to live.

The year before Walsh took over the 49ers, they went 2 and 14. His first year as head coach and general manager, they went . . . 2 and 14. Can you imagine the disappointment? All the changes, all the work that went into that first year, and to end up in the exact same spot as the incompetent coach who preceded you? That's how most of us would think. And then we'd probably start blaming other people.

Walsh realized he "had to look for evidence elsewhere" that it was turning around. For him, it was in how the games were being played, the good decisions and the changes that were being made inside the organization. Two seasons later, they won the Super Bowl and then several more after that. At rock bottom those victories must have felt like a long way off, which is why you have to be able to see past and through.

As Goethe once observed, the great failing is "to see yourself as more than you are and to value yourself at less than your true worth." A good metaphor might be the kind of stock buybacks that Katharine Graham made in the late seventies and eighties. Stock buybacks are controversial— they usually come from a company that is stalled or whose growth is decelerating. With buybacks, a CEO is making a rather incredible statement. She's saying: The market is wrong. It's valuing our company so incorrectly, and clearly has so little idea where we are heading, that we're going to spend the company's precious cash on a bet that they're wrong.

Too often, dishonest or egotistical CEOs buy back company stock because they're delusional. Or because they want to artificially inflate the stock price. Conversely, timid or weak CEOs wouldn't even consider betting on themselves. In

Graham's case, she made a value judgment; with Buffett's help she could see objectively that the market didn't appreciate the true worth of the company's assets. She knew that the reputational hits, the learning curve, had all contributed to a suppressed stock price, which aside from reducing her personal wealth, created a massive opportunity for the company. Over a short period, she would buy nearly 40 percent of the company's shares at a fraction of what they'd later be worth. The stock that Katharine Graham bought for approximately $20 a share would less than a decade later be worth more than $300.

What both Graham and Walsh were doing was adhering to a set of internal metrics that allowed them to evaluate and gauge their progress while everyone on the outside was too distracted by supposed signs of failure or weakness.

This is what guides us through difficulty.

You might not get into your first choice college. You might not get picked for the project or you might get passed over for the promotion. Someone might outbid you for the job, for your dream house, for the opportunity you feel everything depends on. This might happen tomorrow, it might happen twenty-five years from now. It could last for two minutes or ten years. We know that everyone experiences failure and adversity, that we're all subject to the rules of gravity and averages. What does that mean? It means we'll face them too.

As Plutarch finely expressed, "The future bears down upon each one of us with all the hazards of the unknown." The only way out is through.

Humble and strong people don't have the same trouble with these troubles that egotists do. There are fewer complaints and far less self-immolation. Instead, there's stoic—even cheerful—resilience. Pity isn't necessary. Their identity isn't threatened. They can get by without constant validation.

This is what we're aspiring to—much more than mere success. What matters is that we can respond to what life throws at us.

And how we make it through.

ALIVE TIME OR DEAD TIME?

Vivre sans temps mort. (Live without wasted time.)

—PARISIAN POLITICAL SLOGAN

Malcolm X was a criminal. He wasn't Malcolm X at the time—they called him Detroit Red and he was a criminal opportunist who did a little bit of everything. He ran numbers. He sold drugs. He worked as a pimp. Then he moved up to armed robbery. He had his own burglary gang, which he ruled over with a combination of intimidation and boldness—exploiting the fact that he did not seem afraid to kill or die.

Then, finally, he was arrested trying to fence an expensive watch he'd stolen. He was carrying a gun at the time, though to his credit he made no move to fight the officers who had trapped him. In his apartment, they found jewelry, furs, an arsenal of guns, and all his burglary tools.

He got ten years. It was February 1946. He was barely twenty-one years old.

Even accounting for the shameful American racism and whatever systematic legal injustices existed at the time, Malcolm X was guilty. He deserved to go to jail. Who knows who else he would have hurt or killed had he continued his escalating life of crime?

When your actions land you a lengthy prison sentence—rightly tried and convicted—something has gone wrong. You've failed not only yourself, but the basic standards of society and morality. That was the case with Malcolm.

So there he was in prison. A number. A body with roughly a decade to sit in a cage.

He faced what Robert Greene—a man who sixty years later would find his wildly popular books banned in many federal prisons—calls an "Alive Time or Dead Time" scenario. How would the seven years ultimately play out? What would Malcolm do with this time?

According to Greene, there are two types of time in our lives: dead time, when people are passive and waiting, and alive time, when people are learning and acting and utilizing every second. Every moment of failure, every moment or situation that we did not deliberately choose or control, presents this choice: Alive time. Dead time.

Which will it be?

Malcolm chose *alive time*. He began to learn. He explored religion. He taught himself to be a reader by checking out a pencil and the dictionary from the prison library and not only consumed it from start to finish, but *copied it down longhand* from cover to cover. All these words he'd never known existed before were transferred to his brain.

As he said later, "From then until I left that prison, in every free moment I had, if I was not reading in the library, I was reading in my bunk." He read history, he read sociology, he read about religion, he read the classics, he read philosophers like Kant and Spinoza. Later, a reporter asked

Malcolm, "What's your alma mater?" His one word answer: "Books." Prison was his college. He transcended confinement through the pages he absorbed. He reflected that months passed without his even thinking about being detained against his will. He had "never been so truly free in his life."

Most people know what Malcolm X did after he got out of prison, but they don't realize or understand how prison made that possible. How a mix of acceptance, humility, and strength powered the transformation. They also aren't aware of how common this is in history, how many figures took seemingly terrible situations—a prison sentence, an exile, a bear market or depression, military conscription, even being sent to a concentration camp—and through their attitude and approach, turned those circumstances into fuel for their unique greatness.

Francis Scott Key wrote the poem that became the national anthem of the United States while trapped on a ship during a prisoner exchange in the War of 1812. Viktor Frankl refined his psychologies of meaning and suffering during his ordeal in *three* Nazi concentration camps.

Not that these opportunities always come in such serious situations. The author Ian Fleming was on bed rest and, per doctors' orders, forbidden from using a typewriter. They were worried he'd exert himself by writing another Bond novel. So he created Chitty Chitty Bang Bang by hand instead. Walt Disney made his decision to become a cartoonist while laid up after stepping on a rusty nail.

Yes, it would feel much better in the moment to be angry, to be aggrieved, to be depressed or heartbroken. When injustice or the capriciousness of fate are inflicted on someone, the normal reaction is to yell, to fight back, to resist. You know the feeling: *I don't want this. I want* _____. *I want it my way.* This is shortsighted.

Think of what you have been putting off. Issues you declined to deal with. Systemic problems that felt too overwhelming to address. Dead time is revived when we use it as an opportunity to do what we've long needed to do.

As they say, this moment is not your life. But it is a moment *in* your life. How will you use it?

Malcolm could have doubled down on the life that brought him to prison. Dead time isn't only dead because of sloth or complacency. He could have spent those years becoming a better criminal, strengthening his contacts, or planning his next score, but it still would have been dead time. He might have *felt* alive doing it, even as he was slowly killing himself.

"Many a serious thinker has been produced in prisons," as Robert Greene put it, "where we have nothing to do but think." Yet sadly, prisons—in their literal and figurative forms—have produced far more degenerates, losers, and ne'er-do-wells. Inmates might have had nothing to do but think; it's just that what they chose to think about made them worse and not better.

That's what so many of us do when we fail or get ourselves into trouble. Lacking the ability to examine ourselves, we reinvest our energy into exactly the patterns of behavior that caused our problems to begin with.

It comes in many forms. Idly dreaming about the future. Plotting our revenge. Finding refuge in distraction. Refusing to consider that our choices are a reflection of our character. We'd rather do basically anything else.

But what if we said: This is an opportunity for me. I am using it for my purposes. I will not let this be dead time for me.

The dead time was when we were controlled by ego. Now—now we can live.

Who knows what you're currently doing. Hopefully it's not a prison term, even if it might feel like it. Maybe you're sitting in a remedial high school class, maybe you're on hold, maybe it's a trial separation, maybe you're making smoothies while you save up money, maybe you're stuck waiting out a contract or a tour of duty. Maybe this situation is one totally of your own making, or perhaps it's just bad luck.

In life, we all get stuck with dead time. Its occurrence isn't in our control. Its use, on the other hand, is.

As Booker T. Washington most famously put it, "Cast down your bucket where you are." Make use of what's around you. Don't let stubbornness make a bad situation worse.

THE EFFORT IS ENOUGH

> What matters to an active man is to do the right thing;
> whether the right thing comes to pass should not
> bother him.
>
> —GOETHE

Belisarius is one of the greatest yet unknown military generals in all of history. His name has been so obscured and forgotten by history that he makes the underappreciated General Marshall seem positively famous. At least they named the Marshall Plan after George.

As Rome's highest-ranking commander under the Byzantine emperor Justinian, Belisarius saved Western civilization on at least three occasions. As Rome collapsed and the seat of the empire moved to Constantinople, Belisarius was the only bright light in a dark time for Christianity.

He won brilliant victories at Dara, Carthage, Naples, Sicily, and Constantinople. With just a handful of bodyguards against a crowd of tens of thousands, Belisarius saved the throne when an uprising had grown so riotous that the emperor made plans to abdicate. He reclaimed far-flung territories that had been lost for years despite being undermanned and deprived of resources. He recaptured and defended Rome for the first time since the barbarians had sacked and taken it. All of this before he was forty.

His thanks? He was not given public triumphs. Instead, he was repeatedly placed under suspicion by the paranoid emperor he served, Justinian. His victories and sacrifices were undone with foolish treaties and bad faith. His personal historian, Procopius, was corrupted by Justinian to tarnish the man's image and legacy. Later, he was relieved of command. His only remaining title was the deliberately humiliating "Commander of the Royal Stable." Oh, and at the end of his illustrious career, Belisarius was stripped of his wealth, and according to the legend, *blinded*, and forced to beg in the streets to survive.

Historians, scholars, and artists have lamented and argued about this treatment for centuries. Like all fair-minded people, they're outraged at the stupidity, the ungratefulness, and injustice that this great and unusual man was subjected to.

The one person we don't hear complaining about any of this? Not at the time, not at the end of his life, not even in private letters: Belisarius himself.

Ironically, he probably could have taken the throne on numerous occasions, though it appears he was never even tempted. While the Emperor Justinian fell prey to all the vices of absolute power—control, paranoia, selfishness, greed—we see hardly a trace of them in Belisarius.

In his eyes, he was just doing his job—one he believed was his sacred duty. He knew that he did it well. He knew he had done what was right. That was enough.

In life, there will be times when we do everything right,

THE EFFORT IS ENOUGH

perhaps even perfectly. Yet the results will somehow be negative: failure, disrespect, jealousy, or even a resounding yawn from the world.

Depending on what motivates us, this response can be crushing. If ego holds sway, we'll accept nothing less than full appreciation.

A dangerous attitude because when someone works on a project—whether it's a book or a business or otherwise—at a certain point, that thing leaves their hands and enters the realm of the world. It is judged, received, and acted on *by other people*. It stops being something he controls and it depends on them.

Belisarius could win his battles. He could lead his men. He could determine his personal ethics. He could not control whether his work was appreciated or whether it aroused suspicion. He had no ability to control whether a powerful dictator would treat him well.

This reality rings essentially true for everyone in every kind of life. What was so special about Belisarius was that he accepted the bargain. Doing the right thing was enough. Serving his country, his God, and doing his duty faithfully was all that mattered. Any adversity could be endured and any rewards were considered extra.

Which is good, because not only was he often not rewarded for the good he did, he was *punished* for it. That seems galling at first. Indignation is the reaction we'd have if it happened to us or someone we know. What was his alternative? Should he have done the wrong thing instead?

We are all faced with this same challenge in the pursuit of our own goals: Will we work hard for something that can be taken away from us? Will we invest time and energy even if an outcome is not guaranteed? With the right motives we're willing to proceed. With ego, we're not.

We have only minimal control over the rewards for our work and effort—other people's validation, recognition, rewards. So what are we going to do? Not be kind, not work hard, not produce, because there is a chance it wouldn't be reciprocated? C'mon.

Think of all the activists who will find that they can only advance their cause so far. The leaders who are assassinated before their work is done. The inventors whose ideas languish "ahead of their time." According to society's main metrics, these people were not rewarded for their work. *Should they have not done it?*

Yet in ego, every one of us has considered doing precisely that.

If that is your attitude, how do you intend to endure tough times? What if you're ahead of the times? What if the market favors some bogus trend? What if your boss or your clients don't understand?

It's far better when doing good work is sufficient. In other words, the less attached we are to *outcomes* the better. When fulfilling our *own* standards is what fills us with pride and self-respect. When the effort—not the results, good or bad—is enough.

With ego, this is not nearly sufficient. No, we need to be recognized. We need to be compensated. Especially problematic is the fact that, often, we get that. We are praised, we are paid, and we start to assume that the two things always go together. The "expectation hangover" inevitably ensues.

There was an unusual encounter between Alexander the Great and the famous Cynic philosopher Diogenes. Allegedly, Alexander approached Diogenes, who was lying down, enjoying the summer air, and stood over him and asked what he, the most powerful man in the world, might be able to do for this notoriously poor man. Diogenes could have asked for anything. What he requested was epic: "Stop blocking my sun." Even two thousand years later we can feel exactly where in the solar plexus that must have hit Alexander, a man who always wanted to prove how important he was. As the author Robert Louis Stevenson later observed about this meeting, "It is a sore thing to have labored along and scaled arduous hilltops, and when all is done, find humanity indifferent to your achievement."

Well, get ready for it. It will happen. Maybe your parents will never be impressed. Maybe your girlfriend won't care. Maybe the investor won't see the numbers. Maybe the audience won't clap. But we have to be able to push through. We can't let *that* be what motivates us.

Belisarius had one last run. He was found innocent of the charges and his honors restored—just in time to save the empire as a white-haired old man.

Except no, life is not a fairy tale. He was again wrongly suspected of plotting against the emperor. In the famous Longfellow poem about our poor general, at the end of his life he is impoverished and disabled. Yet he concludes with great strength:

> *This, too, can bear;—I still*
> *Am Belisarius!*

You will be unappreciated. You will be sabotaged. You will experience surprising failures. Your expectations will not be met. You will lose. You will fail.

How do you carry on then? How do you take pride in yourself and your work? John Wooden's advice to his players says it: Change the definition of success. "Success is peace of mind, which is a direct result of self-satisfaction in knowing you made the *effort* to do your best to become the best that you are capable of becoming." "Ambition," Marcus Aurelius reminded himself, "means tying your well-being to what other people say or do . . . Sanity means tying it to your own actions."

Do your work. Do it well. Then "let go and let God." That's all there needs to be.

Recognition and rewards—those are just extra. Rejection, that's on them, not on us.

John Kennedy Toole's great book *A Confederacy of Dunces* was universally turned down by publishers, news that so broke his heart that he later committed suicide in his car on an empty road in Biloxi, Mississippi. After his death, his mother discovered the book, advocated on its behalf until it was published, and it eventually won the Pulitzer Prize.

Think about that for a second. What changed between those submissions? Nothing. The book was the same. It was equally great when Toole had it in manuscript form and had fought with editors about it as it was when the book was published, sold copies, and won awards. If only he could have realized this, it would have saved him so much heartbreak. He couldn't, but from his painful example we can at least see how arbitrary many of the breaks in life are.

This is why we can't let externals determine whether something was worth it or not. It's on us.

The world is, after all, indifferent to what we humans "want." If we persist in wanting, in *needing*, we are simply setting ourselves up for resentment or worse.

Doing the work is enough.

FIGHT CLUB MOMENTS

> If you shut up truth and bury it under the ground, it will but grow, and gather to itself such explosive power that the day it bursts through it will blow up everything in its way.
>
> —EMILE ZOLA

There is hardly the space to list all the successful people who have hit rock bottom.

The notion everyone experiences jarring, perspective-altering moments is almost a cliché. That doesn't mean it isn't true.

J. K. Rowling finds herself seven years after college with a failed marriage, no job, single parent, kids she can barely feed, and approaching homelessness. A teenage Charlie Parker thinks he is tearing it up on stage, right in the pocket with the rest of the crew, until Jo Jones throws a cymbal at him and chases him away in humiliation. A young Lyndon Johnson is beaten to a pulp by a Hill Country farm boy over a girl, finally shattering his picture of himself as "cock of the walk."

There are many ways to hit bottom. Almost everyone does in their own way, at some point.

In the novel *Fight Club*, the character Jack's apartment is blown up. All of his possessions—"every stick of furniture," which he pathetically loved—were lost. Later it turns out that Jack blew it up himself. He had multiple personalities, and "Tyler Durden" orchestrated the explosion to shock Jack from the sad stupor he was afraid to do anything about. The result was a journey into an entirely different and rather dark part of his life.

In Greek mythology, characters often experience *katabasis*—or "a going down." They're forced to retreat, they experience a depression, or in some cases literally descend into the underworld. When they emerge, it's with heightened knowledge and understanding.

Today, we'd call that hell—and on occasion we all spend some time there.

We surround ourselves with bullshit. With distractions. With lies about what makes us happy and what's important. We become people we shouldn't become and engage in destructive, awful behaviors. This unhealthy and ego-derived state hardens and becomes almost permanent. Until *katabasis* forces us to face it.

Duris dura franguntur. Hard things are broken by hard things.

The bigger the ego the harder the fall.

It would be nice if it didn't have to be that way. If we could nicely be nudged to correct our ways, if a quiet admonishment was what it took to shoo away illusions, if we could manage to circumvent ego on our own. But it is just not so. The Reverend William A. Sutton observed some 120 years ago that "we cannot be humble except by enduring humiliations." How much better it would be to spare ourselves these experiences, but sometimes it's the only way the blind can be made to see.

In fact, many significant life changes come from moments in which we are thoroughly demolished, in which everything we thought we knew about the world is rendered false. We might call these "Fight Club moments." Sometimes they are self-inflicted, sometimes inflicted on us, but whatever the cause they can be catalysts for changes we were petrified to make.

Pick a time in your life (or perhaps it's a moment you're experiencing now). A boss's eviscerating critique of you in front of the entire staff. That sit-down with the person you loved. The Google Alert that delivered the article you'd hoped would never be written. The call from the creditor. The news that threw you back in your chair, speechless and dumbfounded.

It was in those moments—when the break exposes something unseen before—that you were forced to make eye contact with a thing called Truth. No longer could you hide or pretend.

Such a moment raises many questions: *How do I make sense of this? How do I move onward and upward? Is this the bottom, or is there more to come? Someone told me my problems, so how do I fix them? How did I let this happen? How can it never happen again?*

A look at history finds that these events seem to be defined by three traits:

1. They almost always came at the hands of some outside force or person.

2. They often involved things we already knew about ourselves, but were too scared to admit.

3. From the ruin came the opportunity for great progress and improvement.

Does everyone take advantage of that opportunity? Of course not. Ego often causes the crash and then blocks us from improving.

Was the 2008 financial crisis not a moment in which everything was laid bare for many people? The lack of accountability, the overleveraged lifestyles, the greed, the dishonesty, the trends that could not possibly continue. For some, this was a wake-up call. Others, just a few years later, are back exactly where they were. For them, it will be worse next time.

Hemingway had his own rock-bottom realizations as a young man. The understanding he took from them is expressed timelessly in his book *A Farewell to Arms.* He wrote, "The world breaks every one and afterward many are strong at the broken places. But those that will not break it kills."

The world can show you the truth, but no one can force you to accept it.

In 12-step groups, almost all the steps are about suppressing the ego and clearing out the entitlements and baggage and wreckage that has been accumulated—so that you might see what's left when all of that is stripped away and the real you is left.

It's always so tempting to turn to that old friend denial (which is your ego refusing to believe that what you don't like could be true).

Psychologists often say that threatened egotism is one of the most dangerous forces on earth. The gang member whose "honor" is impugned. The narcissist who is rejected. The bully who is made to feel shame. The impostor who is exposed. The plagiarist or the embellisher whose story stops adding up.

These are not people you want to be near when they are cornered. Nor is it a corner you would want to back yourself into. That's where you get: *How can these people talk to me this way? Who do they think they are? I'll make them all pay.*

Sometimes because we can't face what's been said or what's been done, we do the unthinkable in response to the unbearable: we escalate. This is ego in its purest and most toxic form.

Look at Lance Armstrong. He cheated, but so did a lot of people. It was when this cheating was made public and he was forced to see—if only for a second—that *he was a cheater* that things got really bad. He insisted on denying it despite all the evidence. He insisted on ruining other people's lives. We're so afraid to lose our own esteem or, God forbid, the esteem of others, that we contemplate doing terrible things.

"Everyone who does wicked things hates the light and does not come to the light, lest his works should be exposed," reads John 3:20. Big and small, this is what we do. Getting hit with that spotlight doesn't feel good—whether we're talking the exposure of ordinary self-deception or true evil—but turning away only delays the reckoning. For how long, no one can say.

Face the symptoms. Cure the disease. Ego makes it so

hard—it's easier to delay, to double down, to deliberately avoid seeing the changes we need to make in our lives.

But change begins by hearing the criticism and the words of the people around you. Even if those words are mean spirited, angry, or hurtful. It means weighing them, discarding the ones that don't matter, and reflecting on the ones you do.

In *Fight Club*, the character has to firebomb his own apartment to finally break through. Our expectations and exaggerations and lack of restraint made such moments inevitable, ensuring that it would be painful. Now it's here, what will you make of it? You can change, or you can deny.

Vince Lombardi said this once: "A team, like men, must be brought to its knees before it can rise again." So yes, hitting bottom is as brutal as it sounds.

But the feeling after—it is one of the most powerful perspectives in the world. President Obama described it as he neared the end of his tumultuous, trying terms. "I've been in the barrel tumbling down Niagara Falls and I emerged, and I lived, and that's such a liberating feeling."

If we could help it, it would be better if we never suffered illusions at all. It'd be better if we never had to kneel or go over the edge. That's what we've spent so much time talking about so far in this book. If that fight is lost, we end up here.

In the end, the only way you can appreciate your progress is to stand on the edge of the hole you dug for yourself, look down inside it, and smile fondly at the bloody claw prints that marked your journey up the walls.

DRAW THE LINE

It can ruin your life only if it ruins your character.

—MARCUS AURELIUS

John DeLorean ran his car company into the ground with a mix of outsized ambition, negligence, narcissism, greed, and mismanagement. As the bad news began to pile up and the picture was made clear and public, how do you think he responded?

Was it with resigned acceptance? Did he acknowledge the errors his disgruntled employees were speaking out about for the first time? Was he able to reflect, even slightly, on the mistakes and decisions that had brought him, his investors, and his employees so much trouble?

Of course not. Instead he put in motion a series of events that would end in a $60 million drug deal and his subsequent arrest. That's right, after his company began to fail—failure almost exclusively tied to his unprofessional management style—he figured the best way to save it all would be to secure financing through an illegal shipment of 220 pounds of cocaine.

Sure, after his publicized and very embarrassing arrest,

DeLorean was eventually acquitted on the charges on the rather implausible argument of "entrapment." Except he is on video, holding up a baggie of cocaine, saying with giddy excitement, "This stuff is as good as gold."

There's no question about who caused John DeLorean's disintegration. There's also no question about who made it so much worse. The answer is: HIM. He found himself in a hole and kept digging until he made it all the way to hell.

If only he'd stopped. If at any point he'd said: Is this the person I want to be?

People make mistakes all the time. They start companies they think they can manage. They have grand and bold visions that were a little too grandiose. This is all perfectly fine; it's what being an entrepreneur or a creative or even a business executive is about.

We take risks. We mess up.

The problem is that when we get our identity tied up in our work, we worry that any kind of failure will then say something bad about us *as a person*. It's a fear of taking responsibility, of admitting that we might have messed up. It's the sunk cost fallacy. And so we throw good money and good life after bad and end up making everything so much worse.

Let's say the walls feel like they're closing in. It might feel as if you've been betrayed or your life's work is being stolen. These are not rational, good emotions that will lead to rational, good actions.

Ego asks: *Why is this happening to me? How do I save this and prove to everyone I'm as great as they think?* It's the animal fear of even the slightest sign of weakness.

You've seen this. You've done this. Fighting desperately for something we're only making worse.

It is not a path to great things.

Take Steve Jobs. He was 100 percent responsible for his firing from Apple. Due to his later success, Apple's decision to fire him seems like an example of poor leadership, but he was, at the time, unmanageable. His ego was unequivocally out of control. If you were John Sculley and CEO of Apple, you'd have fired that version of Steve Jobs too—and been right to do so.

Now Steve Jobs's response to his firing was understandable. He cried. He fought. When he lost, he sold all but a single share of his stock in Apple and swore never to think of the place again. But then he started a new company and threw his whole life into it. He tried to learn as best he could from the management mistakes at the root of his first failure. He started another company after that too, called Pixar. Steve Jobs, the famous egomaniac who parked in handicap parking spaces just because he could, responded in this critical moment in a surprising way. Humble for CEOs convinced of their own genius, anyway. He worked until he'd not only proven himself again, but significantly resolved the flaws that had caused his downfall to begin with.

It's not often that successful or powerful people are able to do this. Not when they experience heartrending failure.

American Apparel's founder Dov Charney is an example. After losses of some $300 million and numerous scandals, the company offered him a choice: step aside as CEO and guide the company as a creative consultant (for a large salary), or be fired. He rejected both options and picked something much worse.

After filing a lawsuit in protest, he gambled his entire ownership in the company to initiate a hostile takeover with a hedge fund and insisted that his conduct be investigated and judged. It was, and he was not vindicated. His personal life was splashed across the headlines and embarrassing details revealed. The lawyer he chose to represent him in his lawsuits happened to be the same one who'd already sued Charney close to half a dozen times for sexual harassment and financial irregularities. In the past, Charney had accused this man of shaking him down and making bogus legal claims. Now they were working together.

American Apparel spent more than $10 million it didn't have to fight him off. A judge issued a restraining order. Sales slumped. Finally, the company began laying off factory workers and longtime employees—the exact people he claimed to be fighting for—just to stay afloat. A year later, they were bankrupt and he was out of money too.*

It's like the disgraced statesman and general Alcibiades. In the Peloponnesian War, he first fought for his home country and greatest love, Athens. Then driven out for a drunken crime he may or may not have committed, he defected to Sparta, Athens' sworn enemy. Then running afoul of the Spartans, he defected to Persia—the sworn enemy of both. Finally, he was recalled to Athens, where his ambitious plans to invade Sicily drove the Athenians to their ultimate ruin.

Ego kills what we love. Sometimes, it comes close to killing us too.

It is interesting that Alexander Hamilton, who of all the

---

*I was there and saw all of it. It broke my heart.

Founding Fathers met the most tragic and unnecessary end, would have wise words on this topic. But indeed he does (if only he could have remembered his own advice before fighting his fatal duel). "Act with *fortitude* and *honor*," he wrote to a distraught friend in serious financial and legal trouble of the man's own making. "If you cannot reasonably hope for a favorable extrication, do not plunge deeper. Have the courage to make a full stop."

A *full stop*. It's not that these folks should have quit everything. It's that a fighter who can't tap out or a boxer who can't recognize when it's time to retire gets hurt. Seriously so. You have to be able to see the bigger picture.

But when ego is in control, who can?

Let's say you've failed and let's even say it was your fault. Shit happens and, as they say, sometimes shit happens *in public*. It's not fun. The questions remain: Are you going to make it worse? Or are you going to emerge from this with your dignity and character intact? Are you going to live to fight another day?

When a team looks like they're going to lose a game, the coach doesn't call them all over and lie to them. Instead, he or she reminds them who they are and what they're capable of, and urges them to go back out there and embody that. With winning or miracles off their minds, a good team does its best to complete the game at the highest standard possible (and share the playing time with other players who don't regularly play). And sometimes, they even come back and win.

Most trouble is temporary . . . unless you make that not so. Recovery is not grand, it's one step in front of the other. Unless your cure is more of the disease.

Only ego thinks embarrassment or failure are more than

what they are. History is full of people who suffered abject humiliations yet recovered to have long and impressive careers. Politicians who lost elections or lost offices due to indiscretions—but came back to lead after time had passed. Actors whose movies bombed, authors who got writer's block, celebrities who made gaffes, parents who made mistakes, entrepreneurs with faltering companies, executives who got fired, athletes who were cut, people who lived too well at the top of the market. All these folks felt the hard edge of failure, just like we have. When we lose, we have a choice: Are we going to make this a lose-lose situation for ourselves and everyone involved? Or will it be a lose . . . and then win?

Because you will lose in life. It's a fact. A doctor has to call time of death at some point. They just do.

Ego says we're the immovable object, the unstoppable force. This delusion causes the problems. It meets failure and adversity with rule breaking—betting everything on some crazy scheme; doubling down on behind-the-scenes machinations or unlikely Hail Marys—even though that's what got you to this pain point in the first place.

At any given time in the circle of life, we may be aspiring, succeeding, or failing—though right now we're failing. With wisdom, we understand that these positions are transitory, not statements about your value as a human being. When success begins to slip from your fingers—for whatever reason—the response isn't to grip and claw so hard that you shatter it to pieces. It's to understand that you must work yourself back to the aspirational phase. You must get back to first principles and best practices.

"He who fears death will never do anything worthy of a

living man," Seneca once said. Alter that: He who will do anything to avoid failure will almost certainly do something *worthy of a failure.*

The only real failure is abandoning your principles. Killing what you love because you can't bear to part from it is selfish and stupid. If your reputation can't absorb a few blows, it wasn't worth anything in the first place.

MAINTAIN YOUR OWN SCORECARD

I never look back, except to find out about mistakes . . .
I only see danger in thinking back about things you are
proud of.

—ELISABETH NOELLE-NEUMANN

On April 16, 2000, the New England Patriots drafted an extra quarterback out of the University of Michigan. They'd scouted him thoroughly and had their eye on him for some time. Seeing that he was still available, they took him. It was the 6th round and the 199th pick of the draft.

The young quarterback's name was Tom Brady.

He was fourth string at the beginning of his rookie season. By his second season, he was a starter. New England won the Super Bowl that year. Brady was named MVP.

In terms of return on investment, it's probably the single greatest draft pick in the history of football: four Super Bowl rings (out of 6 appearances), 14 starting seasons, 172 wins, 428 touchdowns, 3 Super Bowl MVPs, 58,000 yards, 10 Pro Bowls, and more division titles than any quarterback in history. It's not even finished paying dividends. Brady may still have many more seasons left in him.

So you'd think that the Patriots' front office would be ecstatic with how it turned out, and indeed, they were. They were also disappointed—deeply so—in themselves. Brady's surprising abilities meant that the Patriots' scouting reports were way off. For all their evaluations of players, they'd somehow missed or miscalculated all of his intangible attributes. They'd let this gem wait until the *sixth round.* Someone else could have drafted him. More than that, they didn't even know they were right about Brady until injuries knocked out Drew Bledsoe, their prized starter, and forced them to realize his potential.

So, even though their bet paid off, the Patriots honed in on the specific intelligence failure that could have prevented the pick from happening in the first place. Not that they were nit-picking. Or indulging in perfectionism. They had higher standards of performance to adhere to.

For years, Scott Pioli, director of personnel for the Patriots, kept a photo on his desk of Dave Stachelski, a player the team had drafted in the 5th round, but who never made it through training camp. It was a reminder: You're not as good as you think. You don't have it all figured out. Stay focused. Do better.

Coach John Wooden was very clear about this too. The scoreboard was not the judge of whether he or the team had achieved success—that wasn't what constituted "winning." Bo Jackson wouldn't get impressed when he hit a home run or ran for a touchdown because he knew "he hadn't done it *perfect.*" (In fact, he didn't ask for the ball after his first hit in major-league baseball for that reason—to him it was "just a ground ball up the middle.")

This is characteristic of how great people think. It's not

that they find failure in every success. They just hold themselves to a standard that exceeds what society might consider to be objective success. Because of that, they don't much care what other people think; they care whether they meet their own standards. And these standards are much, much higher than everyone else's.

The Patriots saw the Brady pick as being more lucky than smart. And though some people are fine giving themselves credit for luck, they weren't. No one would say the Patriots— or any team in the NFL—are without ego. But in this instance, instead of celebrating or congratulating themselves, they put their heads back down and focused on how to get *even better*. That's what makes humility such a powerful force—organizationally, personally, professionally.

This isn't necessarily fun, by the way. It can feel like self-inflicted torture sometimes. But it does force you to always keep going, and always improve.

Ego can't see both sides of the issue. It can't get better because it only sees the validation. Remember, "Vain men never hear anything but praise." It can only see what's going well, not what isn't. It's why you might see egomaniacs with temporary leads, but rarely lasting runs of it.

For us, the scoreboard can't be the only scoreboard. Warren Buffett has said the same thing, making a distinction between the inner scorecard and the external one. Your potential, the absolute best you're capable of—that's the metric to measure yourself against. Your standards are. Winning is not enough. People can get lucky and win. People can be assholes and win. Anyone can win. But not everyone is the best possible version of themselves.

Harsh, yes. The flip side is that it means being honestly

able to be proud and strong during the occasional defeat as well. When you take ego out of the equation, other people's opinions and external markers won't matter as much. That's more difficult, but ultimately a formula for resilience.

The economist (and philosopher) Adam Smith had a theory for how wise and good people evaluate their actions:

> There are two different occasions upon which we examine our own conduct, and endeavour to view it in the light in which the impartial spectator would view it: first, when we are about to act; and secondly, after we have acted. Our views are apt to be very partial in both cases; but they are apt to be most partial when it is of most importance that they should be otherwise. When we are about to act, the eagerness of passion will seldom allow us to consider what we are doing, with the candour of an indifferent person. . . . When the action is over, indeed, and the passions which prompted it have subsided, we can enter more coolly into the sentiments of the indifferent spectator.

This "indifferent spectator" is a sort of guide with which we can judge our behavior, as opposed to the groundless applause that society so often gives out. Not that it's just about validation, though.

Think of all the people who excuse their behavior—politicians, powerful CEOs, and the like—as "not technically illegal." Think of the times that you've excused your own with "no one will know." This is the moral gray area that our ego loves to exploit. Holding your ego against a standard (inner or indifferent or whatever you want to call it) makes it less and less likely that excess or wrongdoing is going to be tolerated by you. Because it's not about what you can get away with, it's about what you should or shouldn't do.

It's a harder road at first, but one that ultimately makes us less selfish and self-absorbed. A person who judges himself based on his own standards doesn't crave the spotlight the same way as someone who lets applause dictate success. A person who can think long term doesn't pity herself during short-term setbacks. A person who values the team can share credit and subsume his own interests in a way that most others can't.

Reflecting on what went well or how amazing we are doesn't get us anywhere, except maybe to where we are right now. But we want to go further, we want more, we want to continue to improve.

Ego blocks that, so we subsume it and smash it with continually higher standards. Not that we are endlessly pursuing more, as if we're racked with greed, but instead, we're inching our way toward real improvement, with discipline rather than disposition.

ALWAYS LOVE

And why should we feel anger at the world?
As if the world would notice!

—EURIPIDES

In 1939, a young prodigy named Orson Welles was given one of the most unheard-of deals in Hollywood history. He could write, act, and direct in two films of his choosing for RKO, a major movie studio. For his first picture, he decided to tell the story of a mysterious newspaper baron who became a prisoner of his enormous empire and lifestyle.

William Randolph Hearst, the infamous media magnate, decided that this movie was based on his life and, more important, that it did so offensively. He then began, and initially succeeded in, an all-consuming campaign to destroy one of the greatest films of all time.

Here's what's so interesting about this. First, Hearst most likely never even saw the movie so he had no idea what was actually in it. Second, it wasn't intended to be about him—or at least solely about him. (As far as we know, the character Charles Foster Kane was an amalgam of several historical figures including Samuel Insull and Robert McCormick; the

movie was inspired by two similar portraits of power by Charlie Chaplin and Aldous Huxley; and it wasn't supposed to
vilify, but to humanize.) Third, Hearst was one of the richest
men in the world at the time, and at seventy-eight, near the
end of his life. Why would he spend so much time on something as inconsequential as a fictional movie by a first-time
director? Fourth, it was his campaign to stop it that secured
the movie's place in popular lore and made it clear the
extent to which his drive to control and manipulate would
go. Ironically, he cemented his own legacy as a reviled American figure more than any critic ever could have.

Thus, the paradox of hate and bitterness. It accomplishes
almost exactly the opposite of what we hope it does. In the
Internet age, we call this the Streisand effect (named after
a similar attempt by the singer and actress Barbra Streisand,
who tried to legally remove a photo of her home from the
Web. Her actions backfired and far more people saw it than
would have had she left the issue alone.) Attempting to destroy something out of hate or ego often ensures that it will
be preserved and disseminated forever.

The lengths that Hearst went to were absurd. He sent his
most influential and powerful gossip columnist, Louella
Parsons, to the studio to demand a screening. Based on her
feedback, he decided he would do everything in his power
to block it from being made public. He issued a directive
that none of his newspapers were to make any mention of
any RKO film—the company producing *Citizen Kane*—
period. (More than a decade later, this ban still applied to
Welles for all Hearst papers.) Hearst's papers began exploring negative stories about Welles and his private life. His
gossip columnist threatened to do the same to each of the

RKO board members. Hearst also made threats to the movie industry as a whole, as a way of turning other studio heads against the picture. An $800,000 offer was made for the rights to the film so that it might be burned or destroyed. Most theater chains were pressured into refusing to show it, and no ads for it were allowed in any Hearst-owned properties. Hearst sympathizers began reporting rumors about Welles to various authorities, and in 1941, J. Edgar Hoover's FBI opened a file on him.

The result was that the movie failed commercially. It took years for it to find its place in the culture. Only at great expense and with great exertion, was Hearst able to hold it back.

We all have stuff that pisses us off. The more successful or powerful we are, the more there will be that we think we need to protect in terms of our legacy, image, and influence. If we're not careful, however, we can end up wasting an incredible amount of time trying to keep the world from displeasing or disrespecting us.

It is a sobering thought to consider for a moment all the needless death and needless waste inflicted over the eons by angry men or aggrieved women on other people, on society, and on themselves. Over what? Reasons that can hardly be remembered.

You know what is a better response to an attack or a slight or something you don't like? Love. That's right, *love*. For the neighbor who won't turn down the music. For the parent that let you down. For the bureaucrat who lost your paperwork. For the group that rejects you. For the critic who attacks you. The former partner who stole your business idea. The bitch or the bastard who cheated on you. Love.

Because, as the song lyrics go, "hate will get you every time."

Okay, maybe love is too much to ask for whatever it is that you've had done to you. You could at the very least try to let it go. You could try to shake your head and laugh about it.

Otherwise the world will witness another example of a timeless and sad pattern: Rich, powerful person becomes so isolated and delusional that when something happens contrary to his wishes, he becomes consumed by it. The same drive that made him great is suddenly a great weakness. He turns a minor inconvenience into a massive sore. The wound festers, becomes infected, and can even kill him.

This is what propelled Nixon forward and then, sadly, downward. Reflecting on his own exile, he later acknowledged that his lifelong image of himself as a scrappy fighter battling a hostile world was his undoing. He'd surrounded himself with other such "tough guys." People forget Nixon was reelected *by a landslide* after Watergate broke. He just couldn't help himself—he kept fighting, he persecuted reporters, and he lashed out at everyone he felt had slighted or doubted him. It's what continued to feed the story and ultimately sank him. Like many such people, he ended up doing more damage to himself than anyone else could. The root of it was his hatefulness and his anger, and even being the most powerful leader in the free world couldn't change it.

It doesn't need to be like that. Booker T. Washington tells an anecdote told to him by Frederick Douglass, about a time he was traveling and was asked to move and ride in the baggage car because of his race. A white supporter rushed up to apologize for this horrible offense. "I am sorry, Mr. Douglass, that you have been degraded in this manner," the person said.

Douglass would have none of that. He wasn't angry. He wasn't hurt. He replied with great fervor: "They cannot degrade Frederick Douglass. The soul that is within me no man can degrade. I am not the one that is being degraded on account of this treatment, but those who are inflicting it upon me."

Certainly, this is an incredibly difficult attitude to maintain. It's far easier to hate. It's natural to lash out.

Yet we find that what defines great leaders like Douglass is that instead of hating their enemies, they feel a sort of pity and empathy for them. Think of Barbara Jordan at the 1992 Democratic National Convention proposing an agenda of " . . . love. Love. Love. Love." Think of Martin Luther King Jr., over and over again, preaching that hate was a burden and love was freedom. Love was transformational, hate was debilitating. In one of his most famous sermons, he took it further: "We begin to love our enemies and love those persons that hate us whether in collective life or individual life by looking at ourselves." We must strip ourselves of the ego that protects and suffocates us, because, as he said, "Hate at any point is a cancer that gnaws away at the very vital center of your life and your existence. It is like eroding acid that eats away the best and the objective center of your life."

Take inventory for a second. What do you dislike? Whose name fills you with revulsion and rage? Now ask: Have these strong feelings really helped you accomplish *anything*?

Take an even wider inventory. Where has hatred and rage ever really gotten *anyone*?

Especially because almost universally, the traits or behaviors that have pissed us off in other people—their dishonesty, their selfishness, their laziness—are hardly going to work out well for them in the end. Their ego and shortsightedness contains its own punishment.

The question we must ask for ourselves is: Are we going to be miserable just because other people are?

Consider how Orson Welles responded to the multidecade campaign by Hearst. According to his own account, he bumped into Hearst in an elevator on the night of the movie's premiere—the very one that Hearst had deployed massive resources to prevent and destroy. Do you know what he did? He invited Hearst to come. When Hearst declined, Welles joked that Charles Foster Kane surely would have accepted.

It took a very long time for Welles's genius in that movie to finally be acknowledged by the rest of the world. No matter, Welles soldiered on, making other movies and producing other fantastic art. By all accounts, he lived a fulfilling and happy life. Eventually, *Citizen Kane* secured its place in the forefront of cinematic history. Seventy years after the movie's debut, it was finally played at Hearst Castle at San Simeon, which is now a state park.

The events he endured weren't exactly fair, but at least he didn't let it ruin his life. As Welles's girlfriend of twenty-plus years said in his eulogy, referring not just to Hearst, but to every slight he ever received in his long career in a notoriously ruthless industry, "I promise you it didn't make him bitter." In other words, he never became like Hearst.

Not everyone is capable of responding that way. At various

EGO IS THE ENEMY

points in our lives, we seem to have different capacities for forgiveness and understanding. And even when some people are able to carry on, they carry with them a needless load of resentment. Remember Kirk Hammett, who suddenly became the guitarist in Metallica? The man they kicked out to make room for him, Dave Mustaine, went on to form another band, Megadeth. Even amidst his own unbelievable success, he was eaten up with rage and hatred over the way he'd been treated those many years before. It drove him to addiction and could have killed him. It was eighteen years until he was able to even begin to process it, and said it still felt like yesterday that he'd been hurt and rejected. When you hear him tell it, as he did once on camera to his former bandmates, it sounds like he ended up living under a bridge. In reality, the man sold millions of records, produced great music, and lived the life of a rock star.

We have all felt this pain—and to quote his lyrics, "smile[d] its blacktooth grin." This obsession with the past, with something that someone did or how things should have been, as much as it hurts, is ego embodied. Everyone else has moved on, but you can't, because you can't see anything but your own way. You can't conceive of accepting that someone could hurt you, deliberately or otherwise. So you hate.

In failure or adversity, it's so easy to hate. Hate defers blame. It makes someone else responsible. It's a distraction too; we don't do much else when we're busy getting revenge or investigating the wrongs that have supposedly been done to us.

Does this get us any closer to where we want to be? No. It just keeps us where we are—or worse, arrests our development entirely. If we are already successful, as Hearst was, it tarnishes our legacy and turns sour what should be our golden years.

Meanwhile, love is right there. Egoless, open, positive, vulnerable, peaceful, and productive.

FOR EVERYTHING THAT COMES NEXT, EGO IS THE ENEMY...

> I don't like work—no man does—but I like what is in the
> work—the chance to find yourself.
>
> —JOSEPH CONRAD

In William Manchester's epic biography of the life of Winston Churchill, the middle volume—a third of the set—is titled *Alone*. For a full eight years, Churchill stood more or less by himself against his shortsighted peers, against the rising threat of fascism, even among the West.

But eventually, he triumphed again. And faced adversity again. And was vindicated again.

Katharine Graham stood alone as she took over her family's newspaper empire. Her son, Donald Graham, must have felt similar pressure as he sought to preserve the company during the dramatic declines of the industry in the mid-2000s. Both made it through. So can you.

There is no way around it: We will experience difficulty. We will feel the touch of failure. As Benjamin Franklin observed, those who "drink to the bottom of the cup must expect to meet with some of the dregs."

But what if those dregs weren't so bad? As Harold Geneen put it, "People learn from their failures. Seldom do they learn anything from success." It's why the old Celtic saying tells us, "See much, study much, suffer much, that is the path to wisdom."

What you face right now could, should, and can be such a path.

Wisdom or ignorance? Ego is the swing vote.

Aspiration leads to success (and adversity). Success creates its own adversity (and, hopefully, new ambitions). And adversity leads to aspiration and more success. It's an endless loop.

All of us exist on this continuum. We occupy different places on it at various points in our lives. But when we do fail, it sucks. No question.

Whatever is next for us, we can be sure of one thing we'll want to avoid. Ego. It makes all the steps hard, but failure is the one it will make permanent. Unless we learn, right here and right now, from our mistakes. Unless we use this moment as an opportunity to understand ourselves and our own mind better, ego will seek out failure like true north.

All great men and women went through difficulties to get to where they are, all of them made mistakes. They found within those experiences some benefit—even if it was simply the realization that they were not infallible and that things would not always go their way. They found that self-awareness was the way out and through—if they hadn't, they wouldn't have gotten better and they wouldn't have been able to rise again.

Which is why we have their mantra to guide us, so that

we can survive and thrive in every phase of our journey. It is simple (though, as always, never easy).

Not to aspire or seek out of ego.
To have success without ego.
To push through failure with strength, not ego.

EPILOGUE

> There is something of a civil war going on within all of
> our lives. There is a recalcitrant South of our soul revolt-
> ing against the North of our soul. And there is this con-
> tinual struggle within the very structure of every
> individual life.
>
> —MARTIN LUTHER KING JR.

I f you're reading this right now, then you've made it
through this book. I was afraid some people might not.
To be perfectly honest, I wasn't sure I'd ever get here
myself.

How do you feel? Tired? Confused? Free?

It is no easy task to go head-to-head with one's ego. To
accept first that ego may be there. Then to subject it to scru-
tiny and criticism. Most of us can't handle uncomfortable
self-examination. It's easier to do just about anything else—
in fact, some of the world's most unbelievable accomplishments are undoubtedly a result of a desire to avoid facing
the darkness of ego.

In any case, just by making it to this point you've struck a serious blow against it. It's not all you'll need to do, but it is a start.

My friend the philosopher and martial artist Daniele Bolelli once gave me a helpful metaphor. He explained that training was like sweeping the floor. Just because we've done it once, doesn't mean the floor is clean forever. Every day the dust comes back. Every day we must sweep.

The same is true for ego. You would be stunned at what kind of damage dust and dirt can do over time. And how quickly it accumulates and becomes utterly unmanageable.

A few days after being fired by the American Apparel board of directors, Dov Charney called me at 3 A.M. He was alternately despondent and angry—genuinely believing himself to be totally blameless for his situation. I asked him, "Dov, what are you going to do? Are you going to pull a Steve Jobs and start a new company? Are you going to make a comeback?" He got quiet and said to me with an earnestness I could feel through the phone and in my bones, "Ryan, Steve Jobs *died.*" To him, in this addled state, this failure, this blow was somehow the same as death. That was one of the last times we ever spoke. I watched with horror in the months that followed as he wreaked havoc on the company he had put everything into building.

It was a sad moment and one that has stayed with me.

But for the grace of God go I. But for the grace of God, that could be any of us.

We all experience success and failure in our own way. Struggling to write this book, I went through four hard-fought but rejected drafts of the proposal and dozens of drafts of the manuscript. On my earlier projects, I'm sure the strain would have broken me. Maybe I would have quit or tried to work with someone else. Maybe I would have dug in my heels to get my way and irreparably damaged the book.

At some point during the process, I came up with a therapeutic device. After each draft, I would tear up the pages and feed the paper to a worm compost I keep in my garage. A few months later, those painful pages were dirt that nourished my yard, which I could walk with bare feet. It was a real and tangible connection to that larger immensity. I liked to remind myself that the same process is going to happen to me when I'm done, when I die and nature tears me up.

One of the most freeing realizations came to me while I was writing and thinking about the ideas in the pages you've just read. It occurred to me what a damaging delusion this notion that our lives are "grand monuments" set to last for all time really is. Any ambitious person knows that feeling—that you must do great things, that you must get your way, and that if you don't that you're a worthless failure and the world is conspiring against you. There is so much pressure that eventually we all break under it or are broken by it.

Of course, that is not true. Yes, we all have potential within us. We all have goals and accomplishments that we know we can achieve—whether it's starting a company, finishing a creative work, making a run at a championship, or getting to the top of your respective field. These are worthy aims. A broken person will not get there.

The problem is when ego intrudes on these pursuits, corrupting them and undermining us as we set out to achieve and accomplish. Whispering lies as we embark on that journey and whispering lies as we succeed in it, and worse, whispering painful lies when we stumble along the way. Ego, like any drug, might be indulged at first in a misguided attempt to get an edge or to take one off. The problem is how quickly it becomes an end unto itself. Which is how one finds oneself in surreal moments like the one I experienced on the phone with Dov, or in any of the cautionary tales in this book.

In the course of my work and my life, I've found that most of the consequences of ego are not quite so calamitous. Many of the people in your life—and in our world—who have given over to their ego will not "get what they deserve" in the sense of karmic justice that we were taught to believe in as kids. I wish it were so simple.

Instead, the consequences are closer to the ending of one of my favorite books, *What Makes Sammy Run?* by Budd Schulberg, a novel whose famous character is based on the real lives of entertainment entrepreneurs like Samuel Goldwyn and David O. Selznick. In the book, the narrator is called to the palatial mansion of a calculating, ruthless, egotistical Hollywood mogul whose precipitous rise he has followed with a mix of admiration and confusion and eventually disgust.

In this moment of vulnerability, the narrator catches a true glimpse into the man's life—his lonely, empty marriage, his fear, his insecurity, his inability to be still even for a second. He realizes that the vengeance—the bad karma—he'd hoped for, for all the rules the man had broken, all the cheating ways he had gotten ahead, wasn't coming. Because it was already there. As he writes,

I had expected something conclusive and fatal and now I realized that *what was coming to him* was not a sudden pay-off but a process, a disease he had caught in the epidemic that swept over his birthplace like a plague; a cancer that was slowly eating him away, the symptoms developing and intensifying: success, loneliness, fear. Fear of all the bright young men, the newer, fresher Sammy Glicks that would spring up to harass him, to threaten him and finally overtake him.

That's how ego manifests itself. And isn't that what we're desperately afraid of becoming?

I'll reveal one last thing I hope will make this come full circle. I first read that passage when I was nineteen years old. It was reading assigned by a seasoned mentor who had found, as I would, early success in the entertainment business. The book was influential and informative for me, just as he'd known it would be.

Yet over the next few years, I worked myself into a nearly identical situation as the characters in the book. Not just summoned to the palatial home to watch the expected and unavoidable dissolution of a person I admired. But to find myself dangerously close to my own shortly thereafter.

I know the passage struck me because when I went to type it up for this epilogue, I found in my original copy pages covered in my own handwriting, written years before, detailing my reaction, right before I had set out into the world. Clearly I had understood Schulberg's words intellectually, even emotionally—but I had made the wrong choices anyway. I had swept once and thought it was enough.

Ten years after first reading it and writing down my thoughts, I was ready once more. Those lessons came home to me in exactly the way I needed them to.

There's a quote from Bismarck that says, in effect, any fool can learn from experience. The trick is to learn from *other people's* experience. This book started around the latter idea and to my surprise ended up with a painful amount of the former as well. I set out to study ego and came crashing into my own—and to those of the people I had long since looked up to.

It may be that you'll need to experience some of that on your own too. Perhaps it is like Plutarch's reflection that we don't "so much gain the knowledge of things by the words, as words by the experience [we have] of things."

In any case, I want to conclude this book with the idea that has underpinned all of what you've just read. That it's admirable to want to be better businessmen or business-women, better athletes, better conquerors. We should want to be better informed, better off financially . . . We should want, as I've said a few times in this book, to do great things. I know that I do.

But no less impressive an accomplishment: being better people, being happier people, being balanced people, being content people, being humble and selfless people. Or better yet, all of these traits together. And what is most obvious but most ignored is that perfecting the personal regularly leads to success as a professional, but rarely the other way around. Working to refine our habitual thoughts, working to clamp down on destructive impulses, these are not simply the moral requirements of any decent person. They will make us more successful; they will help us navigate the treacherous waters that ambition will require us to travel. And they are also their own reward.

So here you are, at the end of this book about ego, having seen as much as one can be shown about the problems of ego from other people's experiences and my own.

What is left?

Your choices. What will you *do* with this information? Not just now, but going forward?

Every day for the rest of your life you will find yourself at one of three phases: aspiration, success, failure. You will battle the ego in each of them. You will make mistakes in each of them.

You must sweep the floor every minute of every day. And then sweep again.

WHAT SHOULD YOU READ NEXT?

For most people, bibliographies are boring. For those of us who love to read, they can be the best part of an entire book. As one of those people, I have prepared for you—my book-loving reader—a full guide to every single book and source I used in this study of ego. I wanted to show you not just which books deserved citation but what I got out of them, and which ones I strongly recommend you read next. In doing this, I got so carried away that my publisher informed me what I had prepared was too big to fit in the book. So I'd like to send it to you directly—in fully clickable and searchable form.

If you'd like these recommendations, all you have to do is e-mail books@egoistheenemy.com or visit www.EgoIs TheEnemy.com/books. I'll also send you a collection of my favorite quotes and observations about ego—many of which I couldn't fit in this book.

CAN I GET EVEN MORE BOOK RECOMMENDATIONS?

You can also sign up for my monthly book recommendation e-mail. The list of recipients has grown to more than fifty thousand rabid, curious readers like yourself. You'll get one e-mail per month, with recommendations from me based on my own personal reading. It kicks off with ten of my favorite books of all time. Just e-mail ryanholiday@gmail.com with "Reading List E-mail" in the subject line or sign up at ryanholiday.net/reading-newsletter.

SELECTED BIBLIOGRAPHY

Aristotle. trans. Terence Irwin. *Nicomachean Ethics.* Indianapolis, IN: Hackett Publishing, 1999.

Barlett, Donald L., and James B. Steele. *Howard Hughes: His Life and Madness.* London: Andre Deutsch, 2003.

Bly, Robert. *Iron John: A Book About Men.* Cambridge, MA: Da Capo, 2004.

Bolelli, Daniele. *On the Warrior's Path: Fighting, Philosophy, and Martial Arts Mythology.* Berkeley, CA: Frog, 2003.

Brady, Frank. *Citizen Welles: A Biography of Orson Welles.* New York: Scribner, 1988.

Brown, Peter H., and Pat H. Broeske. *Howard Hughes: The Untold Story.* Da Capo, 2004.

C., Chuck. *A New Pair of Glasses.* Irvine, CA: New-Look Publishing, 1984.

Chernow, Ron. *Titan: The Life of John D. Rockefeller, Sr.* New York: Vintage, 2004.

Cook, Blanche Wiesen. *Eleanor Roosevelt: The Defining Years.* New York: Penguin, 2000.

Coram, Robert. *Boyd: The Fighter Pilot Who Changed the Art of War.* Boston: Little, Brown, 2002.

Cray, Ed. *General of the Army: George C. Marshall, Soldier and Statesman.* New York: Cooper Square, 2000.

Csikszentmihalyi, Mihaly. *Creativity: Flow and the Psychology of Discovery and Invention.* New York: Harper Collins, 1996.

Emerson, Ralph Waldo. *Representative Men: Seven Lectures.* Cambridge, MA: Belknap Press of Harvard University Press, 1987.

Geneen, Harold. *Managing.* Garden City, NY: Doubleday, 1984.

Graham, Katharine. *Personal History.* New York: Knopf, 1997.

Grant, Ulysses S. *Personal Memoirs of U.S. Grant, Selected Letters 1839–1865.* New York: Library of America, 1990.

Halberstam, David. *The Education of a Coach.* New York: Hachette, 2006.

Henry, Philip, and J. C. Coulston. *The Life of Belisarius: The Last Great General of Rome.* Yardley, Penn.: Westholme, 2006.

Herodotus, trans. Aubrey De Sélincourt, rev. John Marincola. *The Histories.* London: Penguin, 2003.

Hesiod, *Theogony* and *Works and Days* and Theognis, *Elegies.* Trans, Dorothea Wender. Harmondsworth, U.K.: Penguin, 1973.

Isaacson, Walter. *Benjamin Franklin: An American Life.* New York: Simon & Schuster, 2003.

Lamott, Anne. *Bird by Bird: Some Instructions on Writing and Life.* New York: Anchor, 1995.

Levin, Hillel. *Grand Delusions: The Cosmic Career of John DeLorean.* New York: Viking, 1983.

Liddell Hart, B. H. *Sherman: Soldier, Realist, American*. New York: Da Capo, 1993.

Malcolm X, and Alex Haley. *The Autobiography of Malcolm X*. New York: Ballantine, 1992.

Marcus Aurelius, trans. Gregory Hays. *Meditations*. New York: Modern Library, 2002.

Martial, trans. Craig A. Williams. *Epigrams*. Oxford: Oxford University Press, 2004.

McPhee, John. *A Sense of Where You Are: A Profile of Bill Bradley at Princeton*. New York: Farrar, Straus and Giroux, 1999.

McWilliams, Carey. *The Education of Carey McWilliams*. New York: Simon & Schuster, 1979.

Mosley, Leonard. *Marshall: Hero for Our Times*. New York: Hearst, 1982.

Muir, John. *Wilderness Essays*. Salt Lake City: Peregrine Smith, 1980.

Nixon by Nixon: In His Own Words. Directed by Peter W. Kunhardt. HBO documentary, 2014.

Orth, Maureen. "Angela's Assets." *Vanity Fair*, January 2015.

Packer, George. "The Quiet German." *New Yorker*, December 1, 2014.

Palahniuk, Chuck. *Fight Club*. New York: W. W. Norton, 1996.

Plutarch, trans. Ian Scott-Kilvert. *The Rise and Fall of Athens: Nine Greek Lives*. Harmondsworth, U.K: Penguin, 1960.

Pressfield, Steven. *Tides of War: A Novel of Alcibiades and the Peloponnesian War*. New York: Bantam, 2001.

Rampersad, Arnold. *Jackie Robinson: A Biography*. New York: Knopf, 1997.

Riley, Pat. *The Winner Within: A Life Plan for Team Players.* New York: Putnam, 1993.

Roberts, Russ. *How Adam Smith Can Change Your Life.* New York: Portfolio / Penguin, 2015.

Schulberg, Budd. *What Makes Sammy Run?* New York: Vintage, 1993.

Sears, Stephen W. *George B. McClellan: The Young Napoleon.* New York: Ticknor & Fields, 1988.

Seneca, Lucius Annaeus, trans. C.D.N. Costa. *On the Shortness of Life.* New York: Penguin, 2005.

Shamrock, Frank. *Uncaged: My Life as a Champion MMA Fighter.* Chicago: Chicago Review Press, 2012.

Sheridan, Sam. *The Fighter's Mind: Inside the Mental Game.* New York: Atlantic Monthly, 2010.

Sherman, William T. *Memoirs of General W. T. Sherman.* New York: Literary Classics of the United States, 1990.

Smith, Adam. *The Theory of Moral Sentiments.* New York: Penguin, 2009.

Smith, Jean Edward. *Eisenhower: In War and Peace.* New York: Random House, 2012.

Stevenson, Robert Louis. *An Apology for Idlers.* London: Penguin, 2009.

Walsh, Bill. *The Score Takes Care of Itself: My Philosophy of Leadership.* New York: Portfolio / Penguin, 2009.

Washington, Booker T. *Up from Slavery.* New York: Dover, 1995.

Weatherford, J. *Genghis Khan and the Making of the Modern World.* New York: Three Rivers, 2005.

Wooden, John. *Coach Wooden's Leadership Game Plan for Success: 12 Lessons for Extraordinary Performance and Personal Excellence.* New York: McGraw-Hill Education, 2009.

ACKNOWLEDGMENTS

In my previous books, I've tried to make a point of thanking not only the people and mentors who have helped with the book, but also to make it clear how indebted I am to the many authors and thinkers I have relied on over the years. This book would not only not be possible without them, but I also feel incredibly guilty that readers might credit me for insights that originated with other, wiser writers. Anything valuable in this book came from them and not me.

This book would not be what it is without the editing and valuable advice of my editors Nils Parker and Niki Papadopoulos. Steven Pressfield, Tom Bilyeu, and Joey Roth provided critical notes early on that I am very grateful for.

I want to thank my wife, who not only helped me personally during the writing of this book, but was my most dedicated reader. I want to thank my agent, Steve Hanselman, who has represented me from day one. Thanks to Michael Tunney for his help with the proposal, Kevin Currie for his help, and Hristo Vassilev for his excellent research work and assistance. Thanks to Mike Lombardi at the Patriots for his support and insight. Also I owe a debt of gratitude to Tim Ferriss, whose support of my last book made this one possible, and the same goes to Robert Greene, who helped make me a writer, and Dr. Drew, who introduced me to philosophy. I want to thank John Luttrell and Tobias Keller for their guidance and conversations with me during the chaos at American Apparel. I'm not sure if I would have made it, period, were it not for Workaholics Anonymous, both their meeting in Los Angeles and weekly calls.

In terms of places, the University of Texas at Austin Library, the University of California Riverside Library, various running trails (and my shoes), and my home away from home, the Los Angeles Athletic Club, facilitated the actual writing in this book.

Finally, would it be wrong to thank my pet goats too? If not, thanks to Biscuit, Bucket, and Watermelon for keeping things entertaining.

Don't miss this modern classic from bestselling author Ryan Holiday

"Follow these precepts and you will revolutionize your life. Read this book!"
—Steven Pressfield, author of *The War of Art* and *Gates of Fire*

THE OBSTACLE IS THE WAY

The Timeless Art of Turning Trials into Triumph

RYAN HOLIDAY
Bestselling author of *Trust Me, I'm Lying*

"First came Marcus Aurelius, then Frederick the Great . . . and now there's you. This surprising book shows you how to craft a life of wonder by embracing obstacles and challenges."

—Chris Guillebeau, author of *The $100 Startup*

"A book for the bedside of every future—and current—leader in the world."
—Robert Greene, author of *The 48 Laws of Power* and *Mastery*

PORTFOLIO
PENGUIN